WINE MADE EASY

MITCHELL BEAZLEY

EDITED BY **SUSY ATKINS**

WINE MADE EASY

Wine Made Easy
Edited by Susy Atkins

Distributed in the United States and Canada by
Sterling Publishing Co., Inc.,
387 Park Avenue South,
New York, NY 10016–8810

First published in Great Britain in 2006
by Mitchell Beazley,
an imprint of Octopus Publishing Group Limited,
2–4 Heron Quays, London E14 4JP

A CIP catalogue record for this book is available
from the British Library.

ISBN-13: 978 1 84533 247 1
ISBN-10:1 84533 247 4

The author and publishers will be grateful for
any information which will assist them in keeping
future editions up to date. Although all
reasonable care has been taken in the
preparation of this book, neither the publishers
nor the author can accept any liability for any
consequences arising from the use thereof, or
the information contained therein.

Commissioning editor Hilary Lumsden
Managing editor Susanna Forbes
Executive art editor Nicky Collings
Project editor Catherine Emslie
Design Gaelle Lochner
Copy Editor Jamie Ambrose
Proofreader Patricia Carroll
Production Gary Hayes
Index Hilary Bird

Mitchell Beazley would like to thank Susy Atkins,
Fiona Beckett, Simon Woods, and Susie Barrie for
allowing their text from earlier *Wine Made Easy*
series titles to inspire this book. (First published
by Mitchell Beazley in 2002 and 2004: *How to
Choose Wine* by Susy Atkins; *How to Match Food
and Wine* by Fiona Beckett; *Understanding Wine
Labels* by Simon Woods; and *Champagne and
Sparkling Wines* by Susie Barrie).

The publishers would also like to thank Helena
Conibear, Editorial Director of Alcohol in
Moderation (AIM), for her assistance in compiling
the Wine & Health chapter, and for allowing the
use of specific AIM information; and finally, the
wineries who kindly allowed their wine labels to be
reproduced for the Touring the World chapter.

PICTURE ACKNOWLEDGMENTS
All photographs (excluding labels) courtesy of
Octopus Publishing Group and Alan Williams,
photographer, except: p.42 LDPG; p.86
OPG/Adrian Lander; p.124 OPG/Tory McTernan.

Typeset in Angie and Balance

Printed and bound by
Toppan Printing Company in China

CONTENTS

Introduction

Welcome to a comprehensive new book which, quite simply, helps anyone who wants to learn more about the wonderful world of wine. It's not aimed at the connoisseur, but at all those millions of people who have discovered they enjoy this extraordinary, fascinating liquid and want to delve deeper into the facts that surround it. Wine can be an intimidating subject, but not here. This is an easy-to-read, helpful, and informative guide that you'll turn to time and time again.

So many wine books either focus on one aspect of the subject in some detail (*e.g.* a particular region) or they are essentially buying guides with lists of recommended producers. But here, inspired by Mitchell Beazley's *Wine Made Easy* series of handy books on specific wine-related topics, we have drawn together an excellent team of contributors and covered all the bases to create the ultimate guidebook. So you'll find all you need to know about wine styles and grape varieties, and how to buy, store, and serve your wine. There are loads of tips throughout, and chapters devoted to how to read wine labels, wine-and-food matching, and wine and health.

How this book works

The opening chapter brings you straight onto the important business of choosing and buying the right bottle. Here you'll find the low-down on the difference between blends and "single-varietal" wines, and a simple guide, upfront, to the classic styles of white, red, rosé, sparkling, and sweet wines. There is also a useful section on sticking to a budget, buying for special occasions, and choosing where to buy your wine: supermarket, independent merchant, internet, mail order, or at the cellar door. Then, after you've got some tips on buying your bottles, there's a chapter on storing and serving your wine. You've probably wondered whether it's important to serve wine at the right temperature, or if you need to decant it. Here are the answers, with tips on glasses, ageing wine, and creating a "cellar" space in any home.

Next we turn to the often difficult topic of wine labels. How many times have you struggled over a particularly arcane bottle, wondering what the stuff inside actually tastes like? Read Simon Woods's wise words on reading the labels, and not only will you be able to choose a bottle much more easily, but you'll learn a surprising amount about each important wine region in the process.

After that comes an in-depth look at the subject of tasting wine and why it matters to linger over the liquid in your glass. Just what can you get out of sniffing and sipping wine at some length, and which characteristics should you be looking out for? We even tell you how to set up a fun and sociable tasting with friends at home. Then there's a close-up on all the most popular, high-quality grape varieties, with some fascinating facts about each one. We point you toward the flavours and aromas to expect from them all. And no comprehensive wine book would be complete without a good look at a tempting subject: food-and-wine matching. Fiona Beckett has created some extremely useful charts so that you can find great partners at a glance. She has suggested both safe, traditional matches and some more unusual, adventurous bottles to go with each dish.

Finally, you'll also find a whole chapter on wine and health in this book. There seems to be a new report almost every day on whether wine is good for you, and how much you should drink. Some reports are positive, while others can cause us to worry if we enjoy wine regularly. So here you'll find all the latest facts in an easy-to-digest format (no pun intended). This close focus on wine and health is perhaps unique to any general wine book. We hope it is useful.

Do bear in mind that this is a reference book, not necessarily the type that you are meant to read from cover to cover. You might find certain facts repeated here and there because they are pertinent to more than one chapter; no apologies for that. The idea is that you will find what you need easily and quickly when you turn to a particular chapter. And we've made sure there are plenty of cross-references to direct you to other parts of the book which might give you even more information on a subject.

Learning about wine takes a bit of time and an awful lot of tasting (and that part is up to you). But it's great fun – and it's surprising how far a little information can go. Indeed, once you've unearthed a new grape variety, new style of wine, or new wine region, you'll find you're off again, discovering a whole extra branch of the subject. I guarantee that once you start looking up various facts in this book, the whole thing will become infectious. It starts to seem effortless, especially once you put all that new knowledge into practice.

I hope you enjoy this book, preferably with a glass or two in hand, and I hope you start to build on your early enthusiasm to develop a life-long love of the subject of wine.

Susy Atkins

CHOOSING & BUYING

Faced with the huge number of wines in our shops, it can be daunting to know where to start. Should you choose a single-varietal wine or a blend of grapes? What about the New World vs Europe? Which wines offer the best value for money? Here are some essential facts designed to help you decide which styles to buy, where to go for your wine, and how much to pay for it.

Grapes: blend & varietal

Two key issues crop up the moment you glance at the bottles on the shop shelves. Should you buy a single-varietal wine (one made entirely from one grape) or a blend? And what does the huge difference in labels, especially between those from the "New" and "Old World" regions, tell you? Here are the answers you'll need from the start.

Blends vs single varietals

Once you've discovered a grape variety you like, it's tempting to stick with it and ignore the other options. But don't get stuck in a rut, as there are so many flavours and aromas to sample. That goes for combinations of grapes, too. It's a myth that single-varietal wines (100 per cent Chardonnay or 100 per cent Merlot, for example) are always better than blends, although they have been more fashionable recently. In fact, many of the world's greatest wines are blends, and it can be argued that these are more complex and exciting than those made from just one grape variety.

Take Cabernet Sauvignon/Merlot blends, for example. Most top clarets are made mainly from a blend of these two grape varieties. The Cabernet provides structure, power, and a wonderful cassis character, while the Merlot component fleshes out the wine with its generous, plummy fruit and soft, ripe flavours. Grassy, crisp Sauvignon Blanc and fatter Semillon are also often blended together in southwest France, sometimes with brilliant results. The Australians have made powerful, compelling blends of Cabernet and spicy Shiraz, while many of the best sparkling wines in the world are created by splicing the juice of Chardonnay with that of Pinot Noir.

Keep an open mind when choosing your wine and try both single-varietal wines and blends to give yourself plenty of taste opportunities.

What's on the label?

Likewise, try to avoid harsh judgments when looking at the packaging of a wine – the front label in particular. The biggest difference between New World and Old World labels is that, in general, the New World highlights the grape variety, while the Old World puts the emphasis on the region of origin. Familiarize yourself with perhaps a dozen grape varieties (there's much more about grapes later on in the book) and you'll have cracked the basics about most New World wines. As a bonus, these bottles often sport a back label that provides further details about what to expect from the wine, gives serving suggestions, and maybe even includes a pointer to a website for more information.

When it comes to the Old World, informative back labels are more scarce. On the front of the bottles, the most prominent words are place-names, such as Sancerre, Rioja, or Chianti. What can these tell novices about the wine in the bottle? Without help at hand, could they possibly know that France's Châteauneuf-du-Pape, Italy's Cannonau di Sardegna, and Spain's Priorato are all based on the Grenache grape?

While New World labels tend to be simpler than their Old World counterparts, is there a danger of being too simplistic? Certainly. Many people now choose Chardonnay irrespective of its region of origin, almost as if there were just one blend for the entire world. Quality-minded New World producers are aware of this, and now put more emphasis on the region of origin of their wines. Single-vineyard wines are becoming more common as the producers work out how different parts of their vineyards yield wines with distinct characters.

As a result, some New World wine labels are a little more wordy than they used to be, but they still have a long way to go before becoming as complicated as certain examples from Europe. Don't make the mistake of just sticking to these and thinking that simple labels equal good wine, however. Great (and ghastly) wines lurk behind every type of label. It is well worth mastering the more complex labels of European bottles; this book will give you a good grounding in each area of the winemaking world. There's loads more info about labels in the "Touring the World" section on page 42.

White wines

Tired of Chardonnay? It comes in many different guises, so don't give up on it. That said, it's well worth casting around for some white wines made from other grapes. Here are some of the main styles of white that fight for your affections.

The great white grapes

Chardonnay

Chardonnay has taken over the world, stealing the hearts of winemakers everywhere. But not all wine-drinkers feel the same; many Chardonnays are over-oaked and overblown. The ripest and most powerful ones come from hotter parts of California and Australia. More elegant styles are made in Chablis and Italy, while both New Zealand and South Africa tend to produce medium-weight contenders. Chile, eastern Europe, Argentina, and southern France score for great value, but top burgundies rule: they're complex and full of nuts, cream, apples...

ALSO TRY

Viognier – It's peachy, man. Fleshy, floral-scented wines oozing peach and apricot from the Rhône or the New World.

Semillon – Younger versions are grassy and lean, but with age the wines become fatter, lime-juicy, and honeyed.

Albariño – Western Spain's acclaimed white grape makes scented, tangy, and ripe wines for matching with fish.

Chenin Blanc – Tastes of apples and smells of hay. Good Chenin is lovely stuff, but poor examples abound.

Dry vs sweet

Back in the 1970s, medium-sweet whites were fashionable, then bone-dry styles took over. Today, thankfully, anything goes. Problems arise, however, when it isn't clear from the label whether a wine is sweet, medium, or dry. Wines from Alsace are notoriously difficult in this respect, and white Bordeaux has been known to flummox drinkers, too. *See* the glossary on page 159 for some guidance, but trial and error can sometimes be the only solution.

Riesling

Don't make the mistake of equating Riesling with the worst cheap German whites (which are made from inferior grapes); Riesling makes some of the world's best whites. Think apples and pears, delicate orchard-fruit flavours, spine-tingling acidity when young, with softer, richer honey and even petrol aromas creeping in with age. It keeps for years.

ALSO TRY

Gewurztraminer – Gewurz has an exotic aroma of rose petals, ginger, lychees, and Turkish Delight.
Pinot Blanc – No one could argue with such a pleasant wine: fresh, soft, and appley – and highly quaffable.
Pinot Gris/Grigio – Pinot Gris is richer, with a golden colour and smoky, spicy hints. Italian Pinot Grigio is lighter and spritzier.

Sauvignon Blanc

Now very fashionable, whether you prefer the elegant lemons-and-grapefruit style from the Loire, or the deeply aromatic, succulent wines bursting with gooseberry and tomato leaf from New Zealand. Blended with Semillon in southwest France to create grassy whites, both mundane and marvellous. Almost always unoaked.

ALSO TRY

Muscat – Dry wines made from this grape actually taste of, um, grapes: crunchy green ones. A crisp, mouth-watering variety.
Muscadet – A neutral white wine, but zippy and fresh and perfect for washing down shellfish.

To oak or not to oak

White wine aged carefully in oak barrels has an added complexity, structure, and richness, and often displays rich notes of vanilla, butter, toast, and spice. A talented winemaker can get the oak to meld with the natural flavour of the wine, and aims to create the right balance between oak, fruit, acidity, and so on. Some whites really do benefit from oak, and would seem bland and one-dimensional without it. But clumsy, over-oaked whites are out there; avoid those that smell and taste like sawdust and vanilla essence. Only a termite could enjoy such wines, which are often made by dunking oak chips in the vat.

Red wines

Most of us have heard of the grapes Cabernet Sauvignon, Merlot, and Pinot Noir. But have you tasted Nebbiolo, Malbec, or Zinfandel? Throw open the door to other red varieties and you'll experience some exciting new flavours and styles.

The great red grapes

Cabernet Sauvignon

Imagine a deep, rich colour, ripe blackcurrant flavour, firm structure, and aromatic hints of cedar and chocolate. Mature wines have mellow, gamey flavours and a cigar-box aroma. Cabernet Sauvignon is rightly respected. It's often blended with Merlot and Cabernet Franc in Bordeaux (to make claret), Shiraz in Australia, or Sangiovese in Italy.

ALSO TRY

Nebbiolo – Makes firm, powerful Barolo and Barbaresco.
Tempranillo – Rioja's traditionally oaky red, with ripe strawberry and good vanilla character.

Pinot Noir

A real smoothie, Pinot Noir is what lies behind silky, soft, beguiling wines with seductive red-berry flavours. With age, these can become earthy, with an almost manure-like aroma (better than it sounds). Most red Burgundy is Pinot Noir; some great examples also come from California, New Zealand, and cooler parts of Australia. Can be unreliable and expensive, so tread carefully.

ALSO TRY

Gamay – The Beaujolais grape, producing less serious but often juicy, appealing reds that smell like summer pudding.
Cabernet Franc – Raspberry-scented, slightly grassy reds from the Loire Valley. Sip chilled.

Super stoppers

It used to be a very bad sign if your wine was bottled in anything other than glass with a natural cork. Not so today. Screwcaps can be found on good-quality wines, especially Australian ones, and plastic corks have been adopted by many progressive modern wineries. It seems that a lot of us are simply fed up with the huge amount of (natural) cork taint. Even wine boxes seem to contain more palatable booze these days.

Syrah/Shiraz

Fashionable Syrah is behind many of the spicy wines of the Rhône Valley, while as Shiraz, it produces powerful, blockbuster Aussie reds. Not overtly fruity, it often smells and tastes of cloves, chocolate, leather, and black pepper.

ALSO TRY

Grenache – Often blended with Syrah, but on its own it makes fruitier, robust reds in Spain, southern France, and Australia.

Zinfandel – Offers raspberry and black pepper twists. A gutsy red from California.

Merlot

Fleshy, generously fruity reds focusing on sweetly ripe plum, redcurrant, and chocolate flavours. Merlot is often blended with Cabernet Sauvignon (in Bordeaux), providing gentle lushness. Trendy in the New World as a single-varietal wine, the best hail from Chile, California, and South Africa.

ALSO TRY

Sangiovese – With its tangy strawberries and hint of herbs and tobacco, this grape makes seriously good wines, notably Chianti Classico.

Malbec – Contains plenty of black-cherry fruit, usually medium-bodied but smooth. Produces Argentina's most exciting reds.

Does region matter?

A particular grape variety does not taste the same the world over, and one crucial factor is region – climate and soil in particular. For example, red wine from a hot region, such as the Languedoc in southern France, tends to taste a lot riper and richer than red wine from a cooler spot, such as the Loire, even if it is made from the same variety. Increasingly, winemakers across the globe are realizing that they can't just make a wine the way they want it; they have to respect the origins of the grapes and the natural character this gives to the wine.

Rosé wines

Don't miss out on the new craze for rosé. Good-quality rosé tastes so delightfully refreshing, vibrant, and fruity! Try light, subtle, delicate pinks and richly aromatic, ripe, and tangy rosés from around the world.

Australia
Some big and ripe, gutsy rosés are made Down Under, mainly from Grenache. Alcohol levels are higher than usual and there is plenty of rich red-berry flavour. TIP: these more powerful styles can age a bit longer than lighter European rosés.

California
Avoid those "white" or "blush" Zinfandels, which tend to be wimpy, and go for dark pink, vibrantly fruity West Coast rosés, especially those made from Syrah.

France
Reject the popular but fruitless Rosé d'Anjou in favour of raspberry and grass-scented Loire pinks such as Cabernet d'Anjou and Rosé de Loire (mainly Cabernet Franc). Don't miss the Syrah and Grenache rosés from the southern Rhône for richer flavours of rose-hips, redcurrants, and a hint of creamy toffee. Those from Tavel and Provence can be full and ripe, so go well with Mediterranean fish dishes, cold meat, and garlic.

Italy
Italian *rosato* can be excellent: fresh, well balanced, relatively light and crisp from the north; fuller and riper from central regions and farther south. TIP: Carmignano, northwest of Florence, makes some tasty dry pinks, as does Cirò, in Calabria.

Portugal
Once famous for insipid Mateus Rosé, now making a few modern, fruit-driven pinks.

Spain
Bright, vibrant Spanish *rosado* is about as moreish as wine gets. The best come from Navarra and Rioja and have a lively cherry-and-strawberry character.

Staying in the pink
Always chill rosé (still or sparkling) to emphasize its fresh, crisp, succulent qualities. Still versions are rather fragile; their summer-berry flavours don't last long, so drink them while they're young to enjoy them at their best. Rosé's usually light, mouth-watering style makes it perfect for hot summer days, especially with salty tapas.

Sparkling

Wine with bubbles can seem intimidating – there are so many different styles around, yet we feel under pressure to buy the best. Here are some simple facts, at a glance. (There's a more indepth look at the subject in the Wine Styles chapter, pages 125–8.)

Fizz

Chardonnay

Chardonnay has its tendrils in every nook and cranny, including Champagne, where it is one of three grapes that can be used for arguably the best bubbly in the world. It is also used to make sparklers in other French regions and the New World, and even pops up in some modern cavas.

Pinot Noir

Another of the grapes used in Champagne, Pinot Noir is prized for its red-berry fragrance and fruitiness. It is used to make fine fizz in other parts of France and in the New World, where it is almost always blended with Chardonnay.

Pinot Meunier

The third Champagne grape, Pinot Meunier contributes a lively, fresh, and fruity quality to the blend.

ALSO TRY

Riesling – Racy, crisp German, Austrian, and Alsace fizz.

Xarel-lo, **Parellada**, and **Macabeo** – What a mouthful! The Spanish grapes that make easy-drinking, appley cava.

Moscato Bianco (Muscat) – Used to make Asti and Moscato d'Asti in Italy, Clairette in southern France.

Shiraz – In the fun form of curranty, frothy reds from Oz.

Big brands of fizz

Don't always look for a big brand name. If you're buying in quantity for a party, or you fancy a treat but don't want to fork out a fortune, then supermarket own-brands or small-grower Champagnes are a superb choice. They're often half the price of the big boys (who spend oodles of cash on marketing), and they can taste every bit as good, if not better.

Sweet & fortified

Some of the most exciting wines in the world are either sweet or fortified (by adding spirit), or both! These bottles offer concentrated, opulent, rich flavours and aromas. Don't miss out on them.

Muscat

The Muscat family makes a great deal of the sweet wine produced around the world, from light, lemony Moscatel de Valencia to honeyed, floral-scented French *vins doux naturels* and gloopy, toffeed Aussie liqueur Muscats.

ALSO TRY

Semillon/Sauvignon – Responsible for France's great "nobly rotten" (botrytized) dessert wines, Sauternes and Barsac.

Riesling – Also creates superb, complex, sweet wine with crisp acidity, mainly from Germany, Canada, and Austria.

Furmint – The grape which, when nobly rotten, is often behind Hungary's marmalade, honey, and peach-flavoured Tokaji, one of the world's most luscious dessert wines.

Palomino

Palomino produces dull table wine but magnificent sherry. Fino, manzanilla, amontillado, oloroso... all are made almost entirely from Palomino vines grown in Spain's Jerez region.

Touriga Nacional *et al.*

Port is made from a blend of different grapes, but Touriga forms the core of many of the greatest bottles. The small, tough-skinned berries produce a deep colour, lots of tannin, and an intense aroma and flavour of red berries.

What is "noble rot"?

Botrytis cinerea, aka "noble rot", is a disease that attacks a ripe grape, making it shrivel and concentrating the flavours. Wines made from botrytis-affected grapes are unusually gloopy, with naturally high sugar levels, well-preserved acidity, and a delicious character of beeswax, honey, citrus peel, and barley sugar.

New World & Old World

Is there a huge gulf between wines from Australia, California, and so on (the so-called "New World" wine countries) and wines from Europe (the "Old World")? The truth is, there's not nearly as much difference between these bottles as there used to be.

Ten years ago it was usually quite clear whether a wine came from the New World or the Old. First, there was the label (easy to read in the case of NW, often difficult and intimidating in the case of OW). More importantly, the style of wine was often quite different. New World wine was ripe, overtly fruity, and reliably clean and fresh: the result of high-tech winemaking. The best European wines were sometimes more complex and interesting, with distinctive and wide-ranging characteristics due to a larger stash of local grape varieties and more variable climates and vintages. That said, the cheaper wines were likely to show more faults.

Today, wine-drinkers have more difficulty distinguishing New from Old. Why? Let's look back at the recent past and the remarkable rise of Australian wine. In 1975, Aussie plonk was a standing joke. By 2005, it had overtaken French wine sales to become the number-one choice in the UK. Oz and the other New World countries owed their success to good-quality, recognizable, entry-level brands. Today, the main criticism regularly levelled at these nations is that their wines taste a bit one-dimensional and uniform. We think the very worst are over-sweet, over-oaked and over-alcoholic, however "clean", fruity, and consistent they might be. But there's no doubt that New World wines are tremendously popular.

Crossing the wine divide

The Europeans have tried to fight back by cleaning and updating their wineries and introducing more modern methods in the vineyards. Some producers have deliberately made wine in a more fruit-driven, ripe, and rich style, emulating New World wines. Meanwhile, the top New World estates now strive to introduce local or new grape varieties and coax more unusual, distinctive flavours out of them. The result? Overall, better-quality wines, although a less obvious divide between Old and New Worlds.

So what should you buy: Old World or New? The simple answer is: the best of both! Don't rule out any parts of the winemaking globe but do taste as many different wines from as many far-flung areas as you can. For the most exciting flavours of the New World, try smaller producers from smaller regions (Casablanca Valley in Chile, or Margaret River in Australia, say) rather than relying on cheap, cross-regional blends or big brands, which tend to taste disappointingly uniform. When it comes to the Old World, avoid the cheapest wines from the great classic regions like Bordeaux, Burgundy, Tuscany, or Rioja, as these may well not be up to scratch. Better value and more interesting bargains can be found in up-and-coming or underrated parts of Europe.

Sticking to a budget

If you like a particular bargain, good for you. That said, some general advice is useful in determining which wines offer the best value for money.

Bargain basement

Whites
Chardonnay from Chile, South of France, Eastern Europe – Soft, buttery, and ripe.
Touraine Sauvignon Blanc – Better value than rest of the Loire.
Vin de Pays des Côtes de Gascogne – Dry, grassy, and lemony.

Reds
Southern Italy and Sicily – Unusual flavours from local grapes.
South of France – Ripe, rich but soft red wines.
Spain – The cheapest Spanish reds are much improved.

Others
Cava – Spain's wonderfully inexpensive, fresh, snappy fizz.
Sherry – Often ludicrously underpriced.
Rosés – Fresh, young, appealing pink from France and Spain.

Mid-priced gems

Whites
New Zealand Sauvignon and Chardonnay – Wonderfully pure, zesty fruit flavours.
Australia – Try Riesling, Semillon, and Verdelho as well as the ubiquitous Chardonnay.
Chile – Whites are better value in the mid-priced range.
South Africa – Top Chardonnays are remarkably well priced.

Reds
Chile and Argentina – Excellent Cabernet, Merlot, Malbec.
Tuscany – Some fascinating flavours start to creep in.
Rhône – Concentrated, spicy, and firm structure.
Australia – Reigns supreme in this bracket for ripe reds.
South Africa – Single varietals and blends from Stellenbosch and Paarl can be stunning.

Others
New World premium fizz – Especially from New Zealand.
Crémants – France's best sparklers after Champagne.
Fortified wines – Port can be good value, as can serious sherries (dry oloroso, Pedro Ximénez).

Worth splashing out on

Fine clarets (red Bordeaux), white and sweet Bordeaux, red and white Burgundy, vintage Champagne, top German and Austrian Riesling, great Loire whites (sweet and dry), vintage port. The very best wines of the New World – especially Australia and California – are well worth a splurge, too.

Buying for special occasions

The golden rule before buying large quantities is to taste before you buy. Why not invest in several different bottles and have a fun tasting session at home? You'll be glad you spent a little time and money working out which ones are best for your bash.

Weddings

You don't have to have expensive, flashy Champagne at a wedding; a fresh sparkling wine will go down just as well. Pick a lively, fruity fizz from California, New Zealand, or Australia, or a quality *crémant* from France. One solution is to invest in a few bottles of splendid Champagne for the toast, and case-loads of fun New World fizz or Cava for the duration of the party. Table wines for the wedding feast should be crowd-pleasers: soft and fruity. Ripe Vin de Pays d'Oc, Rhône reds, or decent Aussie blends should do the trick.

Dinner parties

Stock up with a dry, unoaked white or fizz as an apéritif, more white (possibly a richer style) and red, of course, for the dinner itself, then consider something different like a sweet or fortified wine afterwards. If you want to serve only two wines, choose a white apéritif wine that suits your first course, too, and pick a red that will go with cheese instead of pudding. Versatile food-friendly wines include: Pinot Blanc from Alsace; lightly oaked or unoaked Chardonnay; Rieslings from just about anywhere; New World Merlot; young Pinot Noir; Rioja *reserva*; Chianti Classico; good-quality mature claret.

Drinks parties

Pick straightforward, tasty bottles that most of your guests will enjoy – not wines with difficult, overwhelming characters. Without food, you won't need heavy, tannic reds, so opt for a softer, lighter style, and avoid whites that are either very acidic and tart or heavily oaked. Try cava; South African Chenin Blanc; New World Sauvignon Blanc; Spanish whites from Rueda; Chilean Merlot; inexpensive Australian Cab/Shiraz blends; good-quality Beaujolais. Don't forget wine boxes and bottles with screwcaps for ease of opening.

How much per person?

Cater for too much rather than too little; if you buy sale or return you won't lose out. Aim over the top, at a bottle per head if you are holding a boozy drinks party, or half a bottle per head for an elegant dinner. Wedding guests tend to drink a huge amount – especially if the party lasts all day and evening – so stock up well!

Where to buy your wine

Armed with all the new knowledge about wine that this book will give you, it pays to move on – perhaps to some different ways to shop for the stuff. Remember to taste as wide a range of wines as you can. That might mean using more than one outlet to purchase your precious bottles.

Supermarket

Buying wine here is easy, and many supermarkets stock a huge range. Special offers can be appealing, too, and turnover is usually fast, so fresh bottles are likely. But these are rarely inspiring places, and the staff aren't exactly wine-wise.

Independent high-street merchant

These shops tend to have a more eclectic and interesting selection. And they often hire staff who know more about the range. Chat up the assistant and find out what's new and exciting.

A specialist merchant

If you've discovered a passion for, say, Austrian whites, or top Burgundy, then try to track down a specialist who has an impressively wide range. A consumer wine magazine or annual "best buys" wine guide may help with this.

Mail order

Wine is undoubtedly a heavy commodity to haul around, so this is a good idea, as long as you go for a well-established, helpful company. Some glossy brochures are much better than others, so look through a few before deciding to buy.

Internet

Surf away, but we recommend using a known and trusted name, not a small, new, obscure website. Expect lots of information on the site. Try to check prices against the local shops before going ahead. Make sure you have watertight arrangements about delivery times – or at least agree a place where wine can be left if you're out.

Cellar door

The best and most enjoyable way of shopping for wine. What could be better than to visit wineries in person, tasting at the cellar door or out in the vineyard and leaving with a case or two of your favourite bottles? Even if you only get a chance to do this on holiday once or twice, do try it – it's inspiring!

Auction house

A number of wine connoisseurs still buy at auction, whether for drinking or simply for investment. Investing in wine is a real gamble, and we'd argue that wine is meant for drinking, not for profiteering! So track down a parcel of seriously good, mature wine and make a bid, which can be a thrill... but we hope you get to sample it, too – not just sell it on.

Vintage or non-vintage?

A vintage wine comes from one particular, named year; a non-vintage wine could be a blend from different years. Most top wines come from very good vintages and if you are planning to splash out on, say, top claret or Burgundy, it pays to mug up on the best years. So invest in a small, recent pocket guide to vintages around the world if you a) intend to buy expensive fine wines regularly or b) want to cellar wine for any length of time, as certain wines made in certain years age better than others. If you are buying inexpensive wines to crack open and enjoy fairly soon after purchase, then don't worry too much about vintages, or indeed about buying non-vintage wine. Focus on other issues, such as a decent producer!

Buying big brands

By all means, stick to wine made by well-known, major producers if you like, as these bottles tend to be fairly safe and reliable. But the big wine brands also tend to be fairly bland – at best, they are crowd-pleasers, but not thought-provokers. In general, it pays to seek out smaller producers and rarer labels for more individual styles and flavours.

Get good advice

Ask for help in a wine shop or restaurant; there should be someone around who can answer your questions (and if not, go elsewhere). Find out which "bin ends" are on special offer; what's new; whether dry sherries or rosés are fresh stock; what matches your dinner dish; what a particular wine tastes like, etc. Why not ask to try something that you intend to buy in bulk? Finally, always return a dud bottle (corked, oxidized, generally substandard). Let's demand more from those who sell wine!

SERVING & STORING

Is it important to store and serve wine correctly? If you are going to drink a particular wine within hours of buying it, store it any way you like. If, however, you intend to keep it for some days or weeks, it pays to know how certain factors may affect its character. As for serving — well, you can always neck it from the bottle on the way home, but that's not going to do justice to fine wine (or do much for your reputation). Here are a few hints, then, on showing your wine in its very best light.

Temperature

There aren't as many rules in the world of wine drinking as some may think, but it *is* crucial to serve your wine at the right temperature. Here's the low-down on which wines should be served chilled (and why) and which are best at room temperature (and why). You may be surprised at one or two suggestions...

Wine is often served too warm or too cold. Sip a too-warm white and you won't get nearly as much succulent "tang" as when it has been chilled. The cold brings out a refreshing, crisp quality in the wine. That said, don't serve light whites and sparklers too frosty, or the flavours and aromas become muted and the wine just tastes bland. A light chill is all you need.

As for reds, never chill a rich, powerful, tannic red wine. Tannins and full-bodied texture just don't taste right cold; these wines usually go with hearty, rich dishes anyway, so chilly vino would not be appropriate. Serve these bottles at room temperature, never warmer – and don't put them by the fire. If they are stored in a cool place, like a cellar, bring them gradually up to ordinary temperature by taking them out well before opening them.

That said, light, soft, juicy reds sometimes benefit from a slight chill. It emphasizes their fresh, fruity quality. It's up to you here; perhaps consider chilling light reds in hot weather, and when pairing the wines with cold food such as ham and salad. But on more bracing days – say, at Christmas parties – leave your light red at room temperature.

Always serve rosés, sparkling wines (both dry and sweet) and dry, pale sherries chilled. Light, golden dessert wines also taste good after an hour or two in the fridge. But rich, fortified wines like ports, sweet Madeiras, and the more luscious dark sherries are generally better when they're served at room temperature. The exceptions here are tawny port and dry Sercial Madeira, which can be served with a chill or without. We recommend cold tawny port with cool chocolate desserts.

Here's a summary

- Chill all whites, sparklers, rosés, and dry, pale sherries for at least an hour (preferably two) before serving. Don't chill them too long, though, or their flavours and aromas will be muted.
- Serve light, soft, juicy reds at a cool room temperature or chill them very slightly to bring out their tangy character.
- Rich, tannic reds should be served at room temperature.
- Serve sweet, rich sherries at room temperature; likewise ripe, red ports. But a mellow tawny is delicious lightly chilled.

Emergency measures

What can you do when you want to chill a bottle in a rush? We've all been caught out this way, and, quite frankly, stirring ice-cubes around in your glass just isn't, er, *cool* (and it dilutes the wine, of course). You could try bunging the bottle in the freezer for a while, but it's all too easy to let it get much too cold in there – or, heaven forbid, to forget about it until it explodes. A much better option is to buy a cheap chiller sleeve which lives in the freezer and can be put around the bottle to reduce the temperature of a wine quickly. If you often find yourself retrieving too-cold bottles from a cellar, you can buy a similar "warmer" sleeve to bring the temperature of a red up. It works by generating heat via a chemical reaction.

One simple way to cool or warm your wine quickly is with an ice bucket. Use ice cubes and water in the bucket to cool wine down, but if you want to warm things up, then it's easy: place the bottle in an ice bucket filled with hand-hot water and leave it there for a few minutes.

You don't need to splash out on a fancy, expensive ice bucket (which might cost a fortune). The aim is simply to keep chilled wine cold, so use anything that's large enough to take some ice-cubes and a bottle. If you're having a big party and need to chill lots of bottles, try filling big, clean plastic buckets and bins with ice. On a picnic, simply dangle the bottle in a pond, stream, or river – even a rock pool – to keep it cool. Tie some string round the end to keep it from plunging to the bottom!

Temperature in restaurants

Reds are often served much too warm in restaurants; if you find that this is the case, send your bottle of hot jam back or ask for an ice bucket to cool it. Any waiter worth his/her salt should understand that warm wine is unacceptable. The best restaurants should offer Beaujolais and other light reds chilled. Likewise, don't put up with whites, fizz, or rosés that haven't been chilled, and expect the waiter to come up with a way of keeping them cool once opened (ice bucket, fridge). Demand to have your wine served correctly, just like your food.

Opening a bottle & decanting

Ever envied the craft of the wine waiter, who opens a bottle brilliantly every time, removing the crumbliest of corks or pouring bubbly without spilling a drop? Here are some tips on opening wine, together with information on why a decanter is not just for Christmas.

Opening the bottle

Picture the scene: you've chosen a wonderful bottle with great care and your best friends are round for dinner. But the cork either sticks as if it has been super-glued to the bottle, or it crumbles into a million little dusty pieces. What a nightmare. It's even worse when the bottle is a particularly fine and old one, as, because corks do tend to deteriorate with age, these are likely to be the most tricky of all. Although there will always be difficult bottles to open (even for the most accomplished sommelier), following some of the tips below should help.

Always remove a cork carefully and slowly, especially if it is old and weak. Watch that wine waiter and you'll see that he never jerks the cork out (or places the bottle between his knees for maximum pull!). Corks should be eased out, especially crumbly ones. For very poor corks, use a simple "waiter's friend" corkscrew (the pocket corkscrew that folds up and has a little knife on the side), making the most of the notches on the side which allow you to lever out the cork very gently. If the cork gives up and breaks, try levering each piece out slowly, removing the cork in sections.

For tough corks that just won't budge, use a different corkscrew. The type with arms that press down to pull the cork out seems to work best with stuck-on corks. There's more on corkscrews on page 35. And if the wine has thrown a sediment, handle the bottle with care so that you don't disturb it too much; pour it out gently, throwing away the muddy dregs (or decant it first – *see* below).

Open sparkling wine and Champagne with great caution. Shaking a bottle of fizz until it explodes is simply dangerous, not to mention wasteful. Never point a Champagne bottle at someone's face. Instead, direct it at a wall, with your hand over it as you remove the wire cage, and aim to ease the cork out slowly with a soft "pssht", twisting the bottle in one hand while easing out the cork gently with the other. Use a dry cloth to grip damp bottles firmly. If you hold the bottle at an angle when you open it, it will be much less likely to gush over and spill.

Decanting

Tannic, young red wine tastes better for some aeration; the air softens and mellows the wine, releasing more aroma and flavour. But the benefits of simply uncorking a bottle an hour or two before serving to "let it breathe" are overrated. When a cork is removed, only a very little bit of wine is in contact with the outside world unless you pour it out. If you want a wine to soften quickly, use a glass decanter. Just the action of pouring the wine into the decanter will expose it to lots of air and immediately change its character. You could get the same effect by simply swirling the wine around vigorously in big glasses at the table, but a decanter is also useful for separating the sediment thrown by some rich reds and ports. Stand the bottle upright for a day or two to let the deposit settle. Pour the liquid slowly and carefully into the decanter until you start to see sediment in the wine; a bright light behind the bottle may help here. A decanter also looks good – it's one accessory every wine-lover should have. How much you use it is up to you. A few wine-lovers swear by decanting almost every bottle – even richer whites – as they prefer the character of a well-aerated wine. Others believe it depends on the context; your tannic, tough red might be perfect with a rare steak, but it may need decanting with creamy, soft cheeses. Experiment with decanting and see what works for you.

Glasses & accessories

We all want fancy glasses and other bits of flash kit when it comes to wine drinking (and especially when entertaining). But don't forget that good wine comes first – so always spend most of your money on that. Here's where to apportion the rest of the budget.

Glasses

Some people get excited about the subject of wine and immediately rush off to buy extremely expensive fancy glasses – maybe cut crystal or coloured glass, perhaps with patterns on the rim or bowl. Big mistake. The very best glasses for showing off fine wine are wonderfully plain, clear, and simple. This is so you can examine the wine's colour and texture easily. After all, the *wine* is what it's about – not the glass, which should simply be the best vessel for the job, and one that enhances the liquid inside it.

Top glasses have a long stem so you can hold them there, rather than getting hot, sticky fingers around the bowl, and they tend to be large, so you can swirl the wine around, releasing its aroma. Patterns or glass swirls around the stem are OK, but stick to plain bowls and rims if you want to concentrate on the wine.

Never fill glasses to the brim, but leave enough space for sloshing the liquid around without spilling it. This enables you to release the aroma. It's also a good idea to half-fill glasses as you then refresh them more often, rather than ending up with slightly stale, warming quantities of wine.

The ideal Champagne glasses are tall, slim flutes, which create long streams of bubbles. Pour the liquid slowly down the insides of the glasses so that it doesn't spill over the edge. The best vessels for sherry are not stingy schooners but normal white wine glasses.

Offering a taste

In a restaurant, you can expect to be offered a taste of wine before the pouring proper begins. This isn't an affectation; it's a chance for you to decide if the wine is in good condition. Don't be intimidated here; give the wine a good swirl, a little sip, and assess whether it's corked or not (*see* page 79). If it seems faulty, send it back and you should get another bottle immediately (taste this one, too). If you're unsure, taste it again, and if it still seems dodgy, ask the waiter what he/she thinks. Good waiters will freely admit to a corked bottle and replace it (after all, it's not their fault). Once you've settled on a bottle, do make sure you can get hold of it to top up glasses yourself. No one wants to be waited on slowly and painfully when it comes to wine. In other words, take charge.

Wine accessories

Wine thermometers, fancy stoppers, and silver ice buckets (not to mention vine-embossed hankies) might make jolly gifts for the wine buff, and if you like them, then fine. There's nothing here that will spoil the taste of your wine, and the sense of occasion posh wine accessories provides is rather nice.

That said, there are only three wine-related gadgets that are essential: a decent corkscrew, a simple foil cutter, and a cooling sleeve. The sleeve lives in the freezer and can be popped round a bottle of white to cool it in minutes – less ostentatious (and less messy) than an ice bucket. A simple foil cutter should be just that: either buy a cheap plastic one with metal blades inside, or find one tucked into the side of your corkscrew.

As for corkscrews, the merits of the "waiter's friend" have already been discussed on page 32. We should add that they are good value for money, too. Always buy one with a decent notch on the arm, which you place on the top of the bottle when the screw is in and use to lever out the cork. Corkscrews with arms that go up when the screw goes in, and are then pressed down to remove the cork, without having to resort to any heavy-duty pulling or tugging, are also pretty good. But best of all are the large contraptions that look like something out of a particularly evil dentist's surgery. These have arms that wrap round the top of the bottle, and a lever that forces the crew into the cork and then lifts it out in a flash. Great if you want to open lots of bottles (or have arthritic or otherwise disabled hands), but be warned: these models come at considerable cost.

Tips on cleaning glasses

Wash wine glasses by hand in very hot water, and avoid using detergent, if possible – especially if serving sparkling wine, as the smallest trace of soap can make a fizz go flat. If you must use washing-up liquid, rinse the glasses afterwards extra-thoroughly. Dry and polish with a clean, soft cotton or linen cloth. Store glasses carefully where they won't get dusty or greasy and give them another quick polish before using next time.

Storing wine at home

For those lucky enough to have a cellar in their home, wine storage will present no problems. A cellar is usually the perfect place to store wine: dark, secluded, still, vaguely damp, and cool.

Why does it need to be all those things?

Darkness is important, as constant bright light gradually affects the character of a wine. Still and secluded count, too – not only because glass bottles are fragile, but also because motion affects wine, so store it away from vibrations and knocks. Cool is crucial. If wine is stored at a warm temperature – or worse, at constantly fluctuating temperatures – it will quickly deteriorate. Ideally, keep it at a steady, slightly chilly 10–12°C (50–54°F). Some humidity is preferable to absolute dryness, too, as it will stop the corks from drying out. And keep the bottles away from strong smells such as white spirit, petrol, or pongy paints, as they can alter wine for the worse. If you don't have a cellar, try to find a space in your house where as many as possible of the above conditions apply.

Good spots

The space under the stairs; an old cupboard in a quiet corner; a dark and disused fireplace; even under the bed.

Bad spots

The garage or utility room (fluctuating temperatures and strong smells); the greenhouse or garden shed (too cold in winter, too hot in summer); the kitchen (too warm at times); the utility room (hot, juddering machines); or anywhere near a functioning boiler or heater.

Creating a storage space for wine

- Try to insulate the spot you have chosen against cold draughts, and turn off any radiators.
- If the room is very dry, keep a bowl of water or a damp sponge in there to add moisture to the air.
- Keep bottles lying on their sides so that the corks don't dry out. Either leave them in their original boxes or store them on wine racks (wooden ones are better than metal ones, which can tear the labels).
- Consider the security of valuable wine and lock it up if necessary. There are specialist wine-storage companies which will hold a valuable collection in secure, appropriate conditions and deliver parcels of your wine to you on request. If you decide to go down this route, do use a reputable, well-established company, make sure your wine is marked with your name and address, and keep plenty of evidence on hand in terms of paperwork, contracts, etc., that proves the wine is yours.

● Finally, if you are storing lots of wine, it's a sensible idea to keep cellar notes to remind you when you bought each batch and when it might be ready to drink. If in doubt, open and pour your wine. After all, it is there to be enjoyed and drunk – not squirrelled away in the dark for ever.

Storing wine as an investment

Don't attempt to store your wine at home if you have bought it as an investment unless you are absolutely sure you have the perfect conditions for ageing your goods. Store fine wine incorrectly and it is highly unlikely you'll see any profit from it. If you're investing in young wine for future sales, then it pays to seek the advice of a storage specialist, most likely recommended by the merchant who sold you the stock; this may well be the merchant itself. But beware of this game: many people have been caught out trying to make a mint from fine wine. The fortunes of a particular winemaker, château, vintage, and even style of wine are likely to change over time, making this a very difficult call. You are more likely to get pleasure out of drinking wine, not selling it, but if you are determined, seek as much expert advice as possible, relying on well-established, reputable, well-known wine merchants. At all costs, avoid new, small, obscure companies making claims for wine investments.

Lay your wine down

If you are keeping a bottle for more than a week or two, then be sure to store it lying on its side. This means that the liquid is in contact with the cork, which keeps the cork plumped up and tight in the neck of the bottle. If you stand the bottle upright for too long, the cork dries out over time, shrinking and letting in air. The result? Oxidized wine.

Ageing

Don't make the mistake of thinking that all wines improve with age.
Many inexpensive wines should be enjoyed as quickly as possible
after bottling. Leave them around for too long and their fragile fruit
flavours and freshness disappear quickly.

That's precisely the reason why some wines you enjoy on your summer holidays taste dreadful
by Christmas. Most labels don't offer a clue as to whether a wine will improve or fade away
with keeping, so it's helpful to have an idea of which styles will last the course.

Wines that won't improve over time
- Almost all rosés, especially light, delicate examples. The deepest rosés keep the best, but in
  general, drink up pink.
- Neutral, insubstantial whites with little character. Try keeping a cheap Frascati or Muscadet
  for long and you'll soon find out why you shouldn't.
- Soft, juicy, jammy reds with little structure. Basic Beaujolais, for example, should never
  be cellared.
- Inexpensive fizz and light non-vintage Champagne. Be spontaneous and crack open that
  bubbly now.
- Dry fino and manzanilla sherry. Drink up soon to capture the fresh, almost salty character
  that is the essence of good dry sherry.

Wines that will keep for a year or so
- Ripe, fruity whites such as New World Chardonnay and Sauvignon Blanc should retain their
  character for several months.
- Medium-bodied, well-balanced reds can cellar well for a year or so, simply softening a little
  and becoming even more accessible with time.
- Rioja *reserva* and *gran reserva*. The ageing has been done in the bodega (winery) so don't
  hang onto it for ever.
- The best non-vintage Champagnes and premium sparklers. Good acidity and depth of
  flavour mean they benefit if stored for a short while.

Wines that improve with age
- Fine German and Austrian Rieslings become honeyed and even petrolly.
- Australian Semillon and Riesling. A few years in bottle bring out some richer,
  lime-marmalade depths.
- Any rich, tannic, powerful red (premium red Bordeaux, Rhône, New World Cabernet Sauvignon
  and Syrah/Shiraz). These soften and mellow with age, emerging smoother and more rounded.

- Fine dessert wines from Austria, Canada, France, Germany, and Hungary become more luscious and opulent and lose sharp acidity as they mature.
- Chenin Blanc from the Loire Valley. Dry, medium, or sweet, the best examples need lots of time to open up and soften.
- Vintage Champagne is often released too early. Preferably drink it at least ten years after vintage – if you can stand to wait that long!
- Vintage port needs a long time to settle down, loosen up, and release complex, deep flavours and aromas.

All of this is rule of thumb, however, as when you drink a wine depends a lot on individual tastes. Some people love very old Champagne for its soft fizz and toffeed hints; others find it flat and disappointingly lifeless. Some prefer Pinot Noir when it's bright, fruity, and cherryish; others enjoy the rich, gamey depths of much older Pinot. So try to work out when and how you like certain styles of wine – always bearing in mind, however, that your dinner guests might not share your tastes!

How long to keep once open?

Once opened and exposed to the air, wine oxidizes and deteriorates, similar to a cut apple turning brown. Light, delicate table wines should be enjoyed within two days of opening, while rich, robust ones may be OK after three or even four. Ports and sherries taste fine for a couple of weeks after opening (sometimes longer), and Madeira keeps for months. Always reseal the bottle between servings and store in a cool, dark place.

Recording

Do make notes about the wine you have tasted – they act as a great reference guide to buying in the future. And if you're building up a serious collection of fine and mature wine, such tasting notes can be invaluable.

Your tasting note needs to be only a few words long, indicating what you liked or disliked about the wine. And do make a record of what you tried it with – either on its own, or with a specific dish and whether the match with food worked. Discovering a delicious food-and-wine partnership is great, so be sure to log it for the future. If you have several bottles of the same wine, it can be especially useful to chart its development; an early bottle of the wine might taste much more tannic and powerful than a more mature and mellow bottle from the same case. Write down when the wine tasted at its best to your palate and remember to take note of your findings.

Some find a scoring system useful: marks out of twenty, say, or a number of stars awarded to wines for overall quality and enjoyment. Don't forget to take price (value for money) into account. Some people buy a special cellar book for recording their tasting notes; this should be laid out especially for the job with spaces to note the name, age, price, and so on of each wine before a tasting note is added. Which is all well and good, but you can use an ordinary notebook almost as easily.

In addition, don't ignore the sometimes lovely wines you drink at other people's houses or in restaurants; the latter can cost a horrible amount, so be sure to remember a good experience. Then again, no one wants to look like a geek, so perhaps leave that huge embossed cellar book at home and scribble a few notes on your napkin instead...

Finally, compare tasting notes with other people as much as possible. This is not so that you can develop exactly the same views as anyone else (taste in wine is every bit as personal as taste in books, films, and music) but it often gives you ideas for what to look out for. That's why informal amateur wine clubs – a bit like reading groups – are so popular these days. And do read as much about wine as you can, using up-to-date books, as the wine world moves on and changes so quickly.

TOURING THE WORLD

The labels on a bottle of wine can tell you so much about what's inside the bottle, and about the culture of the country where it was made. Taking the distinctive marks of labels as a starting point, here's a comprehensive tour of the world's wine regions and what to expect from each as a buyer of wine. You'll never pick up a bottle in ignorance again.

The letter of the law

It would be great if there were just one standard of label the world over. There isn't. Broadly speaking, the information can be split into four categories:

The essential
- Country of origin.
- Quality designation – requirements governing terms such as quality wine or table wine are different in each country.
- Name and address of the bottler.
- Volume of container – in litres, centilitres, or millilitres.
- Alcoholic strength – in degrees or per cent.

The useful
- More precise details of origin – region, town, or village, maybe even vineyard name.
- Name and address of the producer.
- Brand name – we're still waiting for a wine to be called "Travesty"...
- Vintage – a minimum proportion of grapes, usually seventy-five to eighty-five per cent, must come from the specified year.
- Grape variety/ies – info forbidden in some countries, but an indicator of wine style.
- Colour – you'd think this would be essential, but it isn't.
- Sweetness – ditto. In some regions (Alsace springs to mind) often you're not sure whether a wine is bone-dry or halfway to syrup until you open it.

The flowery
- Usually found on the back label.
- Tasting notes – can give vital pointers toward a wine's style, but can dip into the realms of fantasy.
- Serving suggestions – vary from helpful ("try this light, crisp white with simple fish dishes") to sick-making ("serve with good food and good friends").

Rules? What rules?

In some countries, it is illegal to name certain grape varieties on the label, but this doesn't prevent clever producers from giving the odd clue as to what you might find inside the bottle. Portuguese producer Cortes de Cima makes a wine in the Alentejo called Incógnito. What's it made from? The back label reads:

> **S**elect fruit from
> **Y**oung vines, well
> **R**ipened,
> **A**nd hand
> **H**arvested

The note at the base of the label is a Bob Dylan lyric: "To live outside the law, you must be honest."

- Technical information – dates of picking; sugar and acidity levels; duration and temperature of ferments; length of oak-ageing, etc. Great stuff for wine geeks, but can confuse the novice.

The bureaucracy

- Some countries require information on recycling; additives used in winemaking; the number of standard drinks in the bottle; details of the importer.

Quality in the EU

All of the major wine-producing countries in Europe – and most of the minor ones – are members of the European Union (EU). There are certain wine-labelling laws common to all EU countries, plus others that are country-specific. The most important EU-wide regulation concerns a wine's identity, so the label must state whether it is a table wine, a quality wine, or a wine from an intermediate level. A quality wine is sometimes indicated by the letters VQPRD (*vin de qualité produit dans une région déterminée*: "quality wine from a designated area"). However, most countries have their own translations of the categories, as the table below shows. More about the terms can be found in the individual country entries.

	Table wine	Regional wine	Quality wine	Superior quality wine
France	*vin de table*	*vin de pays*	VDQS	AC/AOC
Germany	*Tafelwein*	*Landwein*	QbA	QmP
Italy	*vino da tavola*	IGT	DOC	DOCG
Portugal	*vinho de mesa*	*vinho regional*	IPR	DOC
Spain	*vino de mesa*	*vino de la tierra*	DO	DOCa

Labels for table wines must make no mention of grape variety/ies, vintage, or place of origin. The further you travel up the identity ladder from table wines (that is, the further right you move in this table), the more precise the rules are governing a wine's provenance, permitted grape varieties, and production methods. In theory, the quality should also be higher, but this is not always the case. The appellation laws were originally drawn up to prevent fraud, yet many quality-minded producers now find them something of a strait-jacket. As a result, some choose to take a step down the identity ladder in order to enjoy greater freedom in blending. For example, many *appellations contrôlées* (ACs) in southern France forbid the use of Cabernet Sauvignon. Producers who wish to add some Cabernet simply label their wine as *vin de pays*. For a European wine of genuine "quality", the name of the producer is at least as important as which tier of the quality ladder it comes from.

Burgundy

The Burgundians label their wines according to a hierarchy of vineyard sites developed over several centuries.

At the bottom of the Burgundian quality ladder are the so-called generic wine appellations. These include wines such as Bourgogne Rouge or Blanc, which can come from anywhere within the region. The next rung is comprised of the village wines: Marsannay, Mercurey, and so on. Sometimes the vineyard name will also be shown on the label – Meursault Les Tillets, for example – but unless the words *premier cru* or *1er cru* appear, then the vineyard in question is simply a *lieu-dit*, or named site – *i.e.* not considered in the same quality ranking as those in the following paragraphs.

Enter the *premiers crus*, those vineyards that are considered superior to the regular village sites. The labels bear the village name, the *premier cru* designation, and sometimes the vineyard name:

Chablis Premier Cru Fourchaume, Chassagne-Montrachet Premier Cru La Maltroie. If the label simply says Nuits-St-Georges Premier Cru, then the wine is a blend from various *premier cru* vineyards.

Finally, there are the *grands crus*, whose labels make no mention of the village name. So while you might guess Le Musigny is in Chambolle-Musigny, you'll need a wine book to discover that La Tâche lies in Vosne-Romanée. Choosing can be tricky.

Got all that? Unfortunately, the majority of vineyards in the Burgundy region have more than one owner – which means there isn't just one Clos Vougeot made each year; there are dozens. How can you tell from the label which is a good example, and which is a bad one? You can't. Ah well... that's Burgundy.

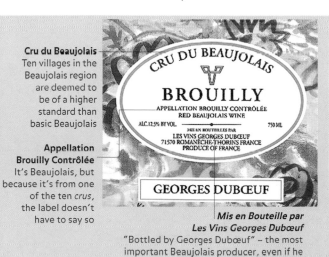

Cru du Beaujolais
Ten villages in the Beaujolais region are deemed to be of a higher standard than basic Beaujolais

Appellation Brouilly Contrôlée
It's Beaujolais, but because it's from one of the ten *crus*, the label doesn't have to say so

Mis en Bouteille par Les Vins Georges Dubœuf
"Bottled by Georges Dubœuf" – the most important Beaujolais producer, even if he has few vineyards of his own

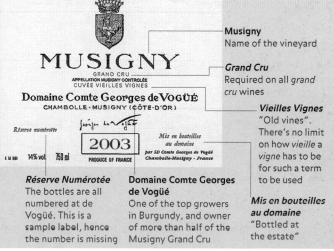

Musigny
Name of the vineyard

Grand Cru
Required on all *grand cru* wines

Vieilles Vignes
"Old vines". There's no limit on how *vieille* a *vigne* has to be for such a term to be used

Mis en bouteilles au domaine
"Bottled at the estate"

Réserve Numérotée
The bottles are all numbered at de Vogüé. This is a sample label, hence the number is missing

Domaine Comte Georges de Vogüé
One of the top growers in Burgundy, and owner of more than half of the Musigny Grand Cru

Bordeaux

After the intricacies of Burgundy, Bordeaux is a little simpler to comprehend.
The typical estate often makes just one wine from one appellation.

In a bid to enhance the quality of this wine, some châteaux (the word "château" has no quality connotations) select only the best batches of wine for their *grand vin*. The remainder is then released as a "second wine"; Les Forts de Latour from Château Latour is an example of this. Some producers even produce a third tier of quality.

There are also fewer appellations than in Burgundy. The generic ACs are the base level, the main ones being Bordeaux and Bordeaux Supérieur – the term *supérieur* indicates a slightly higher alcohol level. Then come some more precisely defined regions: Blaye, Bourg, Médoc, Entre-Deux-Mers, Graves, Sauternes, St-Emilion, Pomerol, and so on. Some are further divided: top Graves wines usually come from Pessac-Léognan; top Médoc reds from Margaux, Pauillac, St-Estèphe, and St-Julien.

Cabernet Sauvignon, Cabernet Franc, and Merlot are red Bordeaux's main grapes, with Malbec and Petit Verdot giving occasional support. Merlot dominates, but in the Graves and Médoc Cabernet Sauvignon has the upper hand. Bordeaux whites are made mostly from Sauvignon Blanc and Sémillon, with perhaps a little Muscadelle.

Rather than remember vineyard hierarchies, Bordeaux fans must acquaint themselves with classifications of châteaux. The most famous, the 1855 classification, divided the top red wines of the region into five tiers: *premier*

grand cru classé, or First Growth; *deuxième grand cru classé*, or Second Growth, etc.

Bordeaux whites were also classified, and everything on the list came from Sauternes or its neighbour Barsac. The three tiers are *premier cru supérieur* (Château d'Yquem is the only one), *premier cru*, and *deuxième cru*. Today, the regions of St-Emilion and Graves both have their own classifications, and there is also a classification of the *crus bourgeois* of the Médoc that grades those properties not included in the 1855 list. These classifications are extensive and, on occasion, controversial, and the comparative price of a wine is often as good an indication of quality as any ranking.

Château Ausone
First-class producer

1er Grand Cru Classé
Could say *premier grand cru classé "A"* because Ausone (along with Cheval Blanc) is considered superior to other *premiers grands crus classés*. The levels below this are *grand cru classé*, *grand cru*, and plain St-Emilion

Appellation St-Emilion Grand Cru Contrôlée
The *appellation contrôlée* name

Famille Vauthier
The Vauthier family owns a number of châteaux in Bordeaux

Alsace

Alsace is unusual in France in that most of the AC wines are labelled according to grape variety. But while this makes Alsace labels easier, its labels are complex in other ways...

While some AC varieties appear elsewhere on French labels, others are confined to Alsace, and one, Klevener de Heiligenstein, is found only in a small district in northern Alsace. Blends can be labelled *gentil* or *edelzwicker*.

Vineyard names appear on some labels, and if the vineyard is one of the fifty *grand cru* sites, the appellation will be Alsace Grand Cru. *Grand cru* wines used to be confined to varietal wines made from Riesling, Pinot Gris, Muscat, or Gewurztraminer, but blends are now permitted.

Champagne

Champagne can come only from the Champagne region of northeast France. It is an *appellation contrôlée* wine, but such is its reputation that the words don't appear on the label.

Vintage Champagne states a specific year on the label, but non-vintage shows no year as it may be a blend from different harvests. Blanc de blancs is made entirely from Chardonnay grapes, and blanc de noirs from Pinot Meunier and/or Pinot Noir. The scale for Champagne runs (from driest to sweetest): brut nature; extra brut; brut; extra dry or extra *sec*; dry or *sec*; *demi-sec;* and finally *doux*.

Small initials on the label indicate the type of producer. You have to look carefully to find RM (a grower), NM (a producer who buys in grapes), or MA (a supermarket or wine merchant's brand name). The numbers that follow these initials identify the producer.

Alsace Grand Cru Just to remind you it's a *grand cru*

Clos Saint Urbain Zind Humbrecht's plot within the Rangen *grand cru*

Rangen de Thann One of the best *grands crus*

Appellation Alsace Grand Cru Contrôlée The appellation

Pinot Gris The grape variety

Domaine Zind Humbrecht A star producer in Alsace

Sélection de Grains Nobles Made from grapes affected by noble rot (botrytis), and so is a sweet wine. If the label says *vendanges tardives*, then the wine has been made from late-harvested grapes and is likely to be off-dry to sweet, and will probably taste richer than ordinary wine

Champagne The only AC wine in France that doesn't carry the words *appellation contrôlée*

Blanc de noirs White wine made from the black/red grapes only: Pinot Noir and/or Pinot Meunier

MA *Marque d'acheteur* – the buyer's own-label, in other words

Produced by Chanoine The company making this particular *cuvée* for UK supermarket Tesco

The Loire Valley

France's longest river, the Loire, is very much white wine territory. Expect labels to show place-names, however, instead of the great white grapes of the region, Sauvignon Blanc and Chenin Blanc.

Le Mont Name of the vineyard

Moelleux "Sweet"

Première Trie The pickers make a number of *tries* through the vineyard to select the ripest, sweetest grapes. The best grapes come from the first *trie*

Huet A fine producer of Vouvray

Vouvray The appellation

East of the mouth of the Loire River is Muscadet. More than eighty per cent of the region's wines come from the Sèvre and Maine sub-region (the other sub-regions are Coteaux de la Loire and Côtes de Grandlieu), and all use the Melon de Bourgogne grape. The best are labelled *sur lie* to show they've been aged on the lees. Cabernets Sauvignon and Franc are used for most Loire reds, and Gamay also appears. Sancerre and Pouilly-Fumé are best known for whites made from Sauvignon Blanc, while Chenin Blanc dominates Anjou-Saumur and Touraine.

The Rhône Valley

The country's other great wine river is dominated by reds, but again, don't expect to see local grape varieties such as Grenache and Syrah on the label; place-names count for everything in the Rhône.

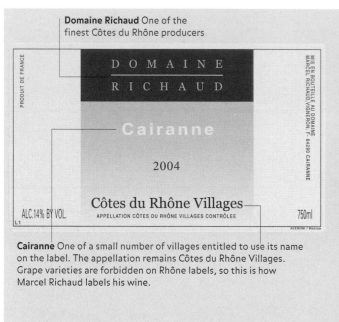

Domaine Richaud One of the finest Côtes du Rhône producers

Cairanne One of a small number of villages entitled to use its name on the label. The appellation remains Côtes du Rhône Villages. Grape varieties are forbidden on Rhône labels, so this is how Marcel Richaud labels his wine.

In the north, the red wines of Côte-Rôtie, Hermitage, Cornas, Crozes-Hermitage, and St-Joseph are usually 100 per cent Syrah; whites are either pure Viognier or Marsanne/Roussanne blends. Farther south, whites tend to be blends of these three grapes plus Grenache Blanc. Many red varieties are permitted for Châteauneuf-du-Pape, Lirac, Gigondas, and Vacqueyras, though they tend to be Grenache-based. Most Côtes du Rhône also comes from the southern Rhône; the word *villages* indicates higher-quality vineyards.

Southern France

Southern France has a number of ACs covering vineyards from the Italian border in Provence to the Spanish border in Roussillon. But only a small proportion of the vast quantity of wine made here qualifies for an AC.

A significant (although declining) amount of rather basic *vin de table* is produced, but, more importantly, there is plenty of *vin de pays*. With *vin de pays*, the regulations are less strict than for AC, so producers can use a far wider selection of grape varieties, plus put their names on the labels. As a result, the range in quality and style is vast, but the grape varieties and the price of the bottle usually provide some indication of what to expect. Wines labelled *fûts de chêne* have been aged in oak barrels. They are more expensive than regular bottlings, but are not always better.

Geographically, *vins de pays* fall into three tiers. First are four regions: Jardin de la France, covering the Loire; Comté Tolosan, covering southwest France; Comtés Rhodaniens, covering central and eastern France; and Oc, covering Languedoc-Roussillon. Then there are the winemaking *départements*, and finally there are almost 100 local designations, though many producers bypass these and use either the departmental or regional names.

The south is also home to most of France's *vins doux naturels* (VDN), made by adding spirit to a semi-fermented wine, yielding a fortified wine with some residual sugar. Look out for Muscat de Rivesaltes, Maury, and Banyuls.

Domaine Piccinini
A consistent performer in Minervois

Clos l'Angély
A single-vineyard wine

Minervois La Livinière
The best sub-region of Minervois

La Baume Sauvignon Blanc
A clean, simple label that will appeal to those reared on New World wines. All the legal requirements appear on the back label (*see page 46*)

Italy – Tuscany and central Italy

Tuscany boasts a number of wines classed DOCG (*denominazione di origine controllata e garantita*). Chianti in its various forms, Brunello di Montalcino, Vino Nobile di Montepulciano, and Carmignano are all exclusively, or predominantly, Sangiovese, while Vernaccia di San Gimignano is the region's sole DOCG white. So are these Tuscany's best wines? Not necessarily...

Many top wines from Tuscany – indeed from throughout Italy – use the *indicazione geografica tipica* (IGT) category, which is similar to the French *vin de pays* category. Just as in France, it is more useful to remember the best wines or producers than the 100-plus IGTs.

DOC (DOCG without the guarantee) Sangioveses to look out for include Rosso di Montalcino and Morellino di Scansano. Other reds of note include Bolgheri (the best-known wine, Sassicaia, has its own DOC) and Val di Cornia with its Suvereto sub-zone. The *passito* (sweet) wine, *vin santo*, which is made in several parts of Italy from grapes picked super-ripe, then allowed to shrivel over a period of a few months before vinification, is at its best here.

Neighbouring Umbria has an increasingly impressive mix of IGTs and DOCs, along with the DOCG reds of Torgiano and Sagrantino di Montefalco. Orvieto, made from Trebbiano and Malvasia, is the best-known Umbrian white (look out for *classico* versions) and a similar blend is used in Lazio for the (in)famous Frascati. The state's best wines, usually red, often appear as IGT Lazio.

Cervaro della Sala Brand name for Antinori's excellent Chardonnay

Umbria This is a single-estate wine, yet it settles for the state-wide IGT of Umbria

Castello della Sala Château Sala, in other words. Other Italian terms for a property include *tenuta* (estate), *fattoria* (farm), and *podere* (smallholding). *Cantina sociale* indicates a cooperative cellar

Chianti Classico The heart of the traditional Chianti region, and home to most of the finest producers

Imbottigliato etc. Bottled at source by the producer

Gaiole Important Chianti Classico village

Riserva More alcoholic and subject to more stringent ageing requirements than the *normale* bottling

The rest of Italy

Here are some of the useful facts about labels from other regions of Italy, starting with the northwest, which means Nebbiolo, the red grape responsible for the majestic wines Barolo and Barbaresco.

Northwest Italy

Barolo and Barbaresco, Piedmont's top DOCGs, are made from 100 per cent Nebbiolo. Neither has any official subdivisions, but many growers mention their vineyard (*vigneto*, *sorì*, or *bricco*) on the label. Those choosing to blend in other varieties use a more general DOC, such as DOC Langhe. Piedmont's other main red grapes are Barbera and Dolcetto, both of which are being treated with increased respect, particularly in the DOCs of Dolcetto di Dogliani, Dolcetto d'Alba, Barbera d'Alba, and Barbera d'Asti. There is a province-wide DOC Piemonte (the Italian for Piedmont) to cover wines that don't fit into other appellations. Asti is more famous for its eponymous DOCG sparkling wine, made from Muscat, and its more refined, less fizzy relative Moscato d'Asti. The northwest has another notable fizz in the form of Franciacorta, made from Chardonnay and members of the Pinot family. To the east, Lugana DOC is a rare decent wine made from the white Trebbiano grape.

Northeast Italy

Friuli-Venezia Giulia and Trentino Alto-Adige make some of Italy's finest whites and, increasingly, fine reds in the DOCs of Colli Orientali del Friuli, Isonzo, Grave del Friuli, and Collio. Grape varieties appear on the labels; look for familiar names (Chardonnay) and local ones like Ribolla Gialla and the red Teroldego. The Veneto is home to the much-maligned Soave and Valpolicella. The best wines, usually from the *classico* zones (the historic vineyards of the region), can be fabulous. Those labelled *recioto* are made from *passito* grapes vinified to produce a decadent sweet wine. Amarone is similar, but is fermented to dryness, while *ripasso* is a halfway house between normal Valpolicella and Amarone. Famed for its Lambrusco, Emilia-Romagna is also home to Italy's first white DOCG, Albana di Romagna, with wines ranging from *secco* (dry) to *dolce* (sweet).

Southern Italy & the islands

The winds of change have blown strongly in southern Italy. Aided by an eclectic portfolio of both international grapes and indigenous varieties (Aglianico, Nero d'Avola, Uva di Troia, Negroamaro, Primitivo, Gaglioppo, and Malvasia Nera for reds, and Greco and Fiano for whites), the wines are improving apace. Some fit neatly into existing DOCs and DOCGs such as Greco di Tufo and Fiano d'Avellino (whites), Taurasi, Aglianico del Vulture, Cirò, Brindisi, and Salice Salentino (reds); others are content with an IGT designation. The name of the producer and the grape variety are more important than the IGT. Sicilian specialties include Marsala (labelled, in increasing quality, *fine*, *superiore*, and *vergine/solera*) and the superb sweet Moscatos and *passitos* from Pantelleria. Sardinia's best wines are reds made from Cannonau (Grenache), Carignano (Carignan), the local Monica grape, and Cabernet Sauvignon.

Germany

German wine labels are an example of a desire to provide information taken too far. Everything you could possibly wish to know about the location of the producer and vineyard, place of bottling, and the district where the wine was officially tested is on there somewhere, either in words or codified in the *amtliche Prüfungsnummer* (AP) number. What the label won't tell you, however, is the quality of the wine.

The definition of the word "quality" is stretched to extremes in Germany, where ninety-five per cent of the wine produced qualifies as "quality wine" (the rest is *Tafelwein* or *Landwein* – see page 46). There are two tiers here: *Qualitätswein bestimmter Anbaugebiete* (QbA) and *Qualitätswein mit Prädikat* (QmP). A QbA might be a fine Riesling from a top estate or an insipid, sickly Liebfraumilch. The price usually tells you what to expect.

QmP wines are categorized according to the must weights (sugar levels) of the grapes at harvest. The basis for this method is that the best vineyards will produce the ripest, sweetest, and therefore best, grapes. The idea falls down with grape varieties that have been developed for easy ripening in the marginal conditions of some German vineyards. The must weights might be high, but the quality often isn't. The levels in the Prädikat system are: Kabinett, then Spätlese (late-picked), Auslese (selected bunches), Beerenauslese (selected grapes), and Trockenbeerenauslese (selected grapes that have been shrivelled by noble rot). For each level, there is a minimum must weight, dependent on the region and grape variety. Some growers make wines from grapes that have been left on the vine until the grapes freeze. Providing the must weight is at least of Beerenauslese level, they can be called Eiswein.

Mosel-Saar-Ruwer is best known for its delicate, racy Rieslings. Don't be surprised to see alcohol levels as low as seven

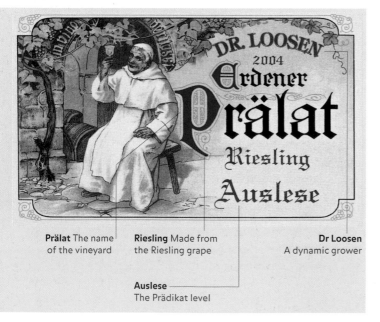

Prälat The name of the vineyard

Riesling Made from the Riesling grape

Auslese The Prädikat level

Dr Loosen A dynamic grower

and a half per cent. This is close to the northern limit of viticulture, and the acidity level in the grapes is high. To balance this, growers often stop the fermentation before all the sugar has turned to alcohol.

It's warmer in the Rheingau than in the Mosel-Saar-Ruwer and, as a result, potential alcohol levels are higher while acidity is lower. With less need for residual sugar in the wines, the tendency today is to make *halbtrocken* (medium-dry) or *trocken* (dry) wines. Sweet wines are usually made solely from grapes affected by noble rot. Several growers still bottle a number of wines at different Prädikat levels from the same vineyard, with some even producing three or four different bottlings of the same quality. They can use the number of a cask (*Fuder*), a gold capsule (*Goldkapsel*), or, better still, a long gold capsule (*lange Goldkapsel*) over the cork to distinguish between them. There is also a move among growers to

highlight only their best vineyard sites – *erstes Gewächs* (First Growth) or *großes Gewächs* (Great Growth), depending on the region – on bottles. Wines from lesser vineyards are used in blends labelled varietally, with Prädikat level and the grower's name. Another effort to simplify German labels is the introduction of Classic and Selection wines. These are dry varietal wines that meet certain ripeness and quality criteria, with Selection being the higher level.

Riesling is Germany's main, but not only, quality grape. Scheurebe, Silvaner, Rieslaner, and Gewürztraminer can all be excellent, as can wines made from members of the Pinot family: Pinot Blanc (Weisser Burgunder), Pinot Gris (Grauburgunder), and Pinot Noir (Spätburgunder). Some of the Spätburgunders are world-class, although many can claim only QbA status because they have been chaptalized (had sugar added to boost the alcohol level).

Weingut Wöhrwag
Wöhrwag Estate

Spätburgunder Trocken
Dry Pinot Noir

Untertürkheimer Herzogenberg
The vineyard name is mentioned, but only in small letters. More is made of the grape variety

Qualitätswein A QbA, because the wine has probably been chaptalized

Gutsabfüllung
Indicates that a wine is estate-bottled; the word *Erzeugerabfüllung* is also used

Württemberg Large but little-known region specializing in red wines

Joe Stefanelli 94

Georg Breuer
A leading Rheingau producer of great wines with simple, stylish labels

Berg Schlossberg
The vineyard

Spain – Rioja & the rest of northern Spain

In Spain, producers are not rebelling against the country's DO system (*denominación de origen*), but against the traditions of blending and ageing wines. This is especially true of Rioja, where many winemakers feel constrained by DO rules on grape varieties and barrel-ageing.

In Rioja, Spain's only DOCa (the "Ca" stands for calificada), Tempranillo is the dominant grape, aided by Garnacha (Grenache), Mazuelo (Carignan), Graciano, and Cabernet Sauvignon. Viura (Macabeo) dominates production of white Rioja, some of which is fermentado en barrica (barrel-fermented).

Like many Spanish wines, Rioja is classified according to the length of ageing. A wine aged for at least two years (one in barrel, one in bottle) is labelled *crianza*. A *reserva* is three years old (at least one in barrel and one in bottle), and a *gran reserva* must be five years old (at least two in barrel and two in bottle). Traditional Rioja is a blended wine from diverse vineyards, but single-vineyard wines are now being made (the terms *viña* and *viñedo* indicate the vineyard name), often with little mention made of the length of ageing.

Navarra uses similar red grapes plus Merlot for its reds and *rosados* (rosés). As Tinto Fino, Tempranillo is also responsible for the highly rated wines of Ribera del Duero. The nearby DOs of Toro and Cigales are also making promising Tempranillo.

A lone outpost of quality white wine in northern central Spain is Rueda, where both Sauvignon Blanc and Verdejo are being used to good effect. Farther west in Galicia, Rías Baixas also excels with whites made from the fragrant Albariño grape, while the pick of the reds is Bierzo, made from the aromatic Mencía variety.

Catalonia is home of cava, made by the traditional method (as in Champagne). Historically it has been made from Parellada, Xarel-lo, and Macabeo grapes, but Chardonnay and Pinot Noir are being increasingly planted. This is also the place for some of Spain's finest, richest reds from Priorato using old-vine Cariñena and Garnacha with more recent plantings of Cabernet Sauvignon, Syrah, and Merlot.

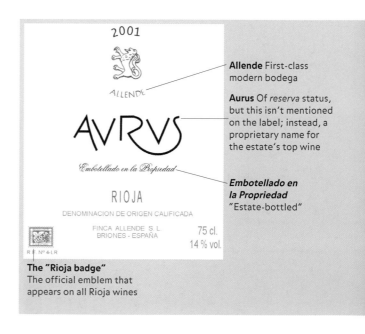

Allende First-class modern bodega

Aurus Of *reserva* status, but this isn't mentioned on the label; instead, a proprietary name for the estate's top wine

Embotellado en la Propriedad "Estate-bottled"

The "Rioja badge" The official emblem that appears on all Rioja wines

Spain – central & southern

Farther south, La Mancha is the source of large amounts of plonk, as well as more ambitious Tempranillo and Cabernet-based reds. Look out, too, for the gutsy Jumilla reds, made from Monastrell (Mourvèdre).

Valencia is enjoying some success with table wines, but is better known as the home of one of the world's best-value dessert wines, Moscatel de Valencia. Finer, but rarer, sweet wines are found on the south coast in Málaga. Various styles are made using Moscatel and Pedro Ximénez (PX), from unfortified *passito* (*see* page 52) to fortified wines similar to the *vins doux naturels* of Roussillon (*see* page 51).

In the sherry vineyards between Seville and Cádiz, the rather neutral Palomino grape is transformed through an intricate blending system called a *solera* into something special. Through the action of a yeasty growth called *flor*, the lightest wines of the region become finos (in Jerez and Puerto de Santa María) and manzanillas (in Sanlúcar de Barrameda).

Olorosos are fuller-bodied, while palo cortado sits halfway between these two styles. In amontillados, the *flor* has died on a fino, and the wine has continued ageing in barrel, though inferior versions (and cream and pale cream sherries) are sweetened olorosos. The finest sweet sherries are olorosos bolstered by some *passito*-style Pedro Ximénez grapes (PX), and a few bodegas even make superb, raisiny wine exclusively from PX.

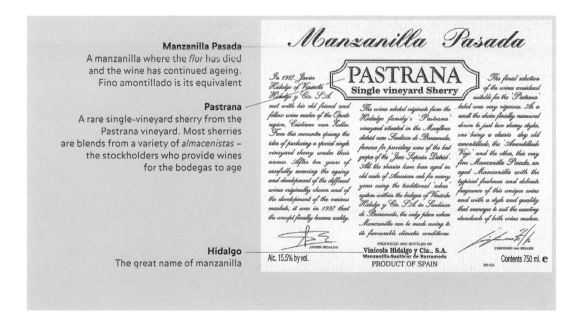

Manzanilla Pasada
A manzanilla where the *flor* has died and the wine has continued ageing. Fino amontillado is its equivalent

Pastrana
A rare single-vineyard sherry from the Pastrana vineyard. Most sherries are blends from a variety of *almacenistas* – the stockholders who provide wines for the bodegas to age

Hidalgo
The great name of manzanilla

Portugal

Portugal's best-known wine is port from the Douro Valley east of Oporto. The red versions (there is white, too) fall into two broad types: ruby and tawny.

Northern Portugal

Ruby ports are bottled young. Vintage port is a wine from a good vintage typically bottled after two years in barrel. Late-bottled vintage (LBV) spends up to six years in barrel. LBVs labelled "traditional" will continue to age in bottle after release. Basic "ruby" is usually a blend from recent vintages. "Vintage character" is simply a higher-quality port. Tawny ports spend much longer in barrels, "breathing" through the sides of the cask and acquiring their tawny hue. Superior tawnies often carry an indication of their age. A tawny from a single vintage is called a *colheita*.

Unfortified wines made in the Douro DOC can also be excellent. Most are blends, but varietal bottlings (Touriga Nacional, in particular) are increasing. Other noteworthy red wine regions in the north are Bairrada, with wine made mostly from the thick-skinned Baga grape, and Dão, made mainly from a cocktail of varieties. Bottles labelled *garrafeira* indicate a producer's special reserve bottling. Northern Portugal is also home to Vinho Verde: *verde* meaning "young" in this case. While nearly half the output is red (*tinto*), the crisp white (*branco*) versions are the most commonly seen outside the country.

Southern Portugal

Port isn't Portugal's only great fortified wine. Off the coast of Africa lies Madeira and its famous eponymous wine. Most is made from the undistinguished Tinta Negra Mole grape, but the best carry the name of the grape variety. Madeira wines can only be labelled according to their average age (three-year-old, five-year-old, etc.) and their sweetness level: dry, medium-dry, medium-sweet, rich, or sweet. The richest and sweetest is Malmsey (Malvasia), then comes Bual, Verdelho, and finally the searing Sercial. Most wines are blends of different vintages, although vintage Madeira can be found; this has a minimum of twenty years in cask. Some vintage wines with less cask-age are bottled as *colheitas*.

Table wines from regions around Lisbon can be good, and are often labelled by grape variety. Wines using non-Portuguese grapes appear as VR (*vinho regional*) rather than DOC. In the Alentejo, where many exciting new wines are made, the producer name is more important. Much wine comes from large co-ops (*adegas*) but there are plenty of progressive small estates, too.

Porto Port doesn't have to mention that it is DOC

Niepoort Small, high-class family firm

Colheita A vintage-dated tawny. The label shows that it has spent nearly fourteen years in barrel before bottling

Other European countries

Though their labels can be tricky to read, Austria, Hungary, and Greece can produce the odd gem. Learn to tell your Gruner Veltliners from your aszú...

Austria

In Austria, as in Germany, wines are classified from Kabinett up to Trockenbeerenauslese and Eiswein, but with an extra category called Ausbruch (between Beerenauslese and Trockenbeerenauslese in terms of sweetness). And the Wachau region also has its own three-tier scale for dry Rieslings and Grüner Veltliners: Steinfeder (the lightest), then Federspiel, then Smaragd. Other terms used include *Ried* (vineyard), *alte Reben* (old vines), Morillon (Chardonnay), Sämling 88 (Scheurebe), and *Schilfwein* (a *passito* style, *see* page 52).

Hungary

Hungary's most important contribution to the world of wine, Tokaji or Tokay (Tokaj is the region), is mostly *szamarodni*, meaning "as it comes", but dry (*száraz*) and sweet (*edes*) versions exist. The real glories are the sweet *aszú* wines. *Aszú* is a sticky ultra-ripe grape paste, and the wines are graded according to how much of this is in the blend. This is measured in *puttonyos* – literally "buckets". The more *puttonyos*, the sweeter the wine. "*Aszú eszencia*" is a seven- or eight-*puttonyos* wine.

Greece

Terms you may find on Greek labels – when you're lucky enough to have a translation of the Greek script – are "Ktima" (estate) and "Cava" (a blend, usually aged). The best local grapes are the white Assyrtiko (best in Santorini) and the red Agiorgitiko/St George (Nemea is the best), Mavrodaphne (good for port-style wines) and Xynomavro (similar to Nebbiolo, look for Naoussa). And Greek versions of Muscat, especially from Samos, can be superb.

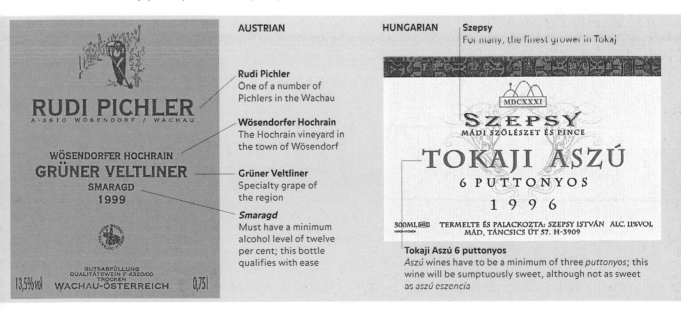

AUSTRIAN

Rudi Pichler
One of a number of Pichlers in the Wachau

Wösendorfer Hochrain
The Hochrain vineyard in the town of Wösendorf

Grüner Veltliner
Specialty grape of the region

Smaragd
Must have a minimum alcohol level of twelve per cent; this bottle qualifies with ease

HUNGARIAN

Szepsy
For many, the finest grower in Tokaj

Tokaji Aszú 6 puttonyos
Aszú wines have to be a minimum of three *puttonyos*; this wine will be sumptuously sweet, although not as sweet as *aszú eszencia*

North America

North America was the first New World country to embrace the concept of varietal wines. The craze began with Cabernet Sauvignon and Chardonnay, but now includes a range of varieties.

The grape variety is a main factor in most people's choice of American wines, but there's growing interest in the origin of wines. There are nearly 150 American Viticultural Areas (AVAs), some covering vast areas and several wineries, others just one or two producers. Their boundaries are geographical or political. The term "AVA" doesn't have to appear on a bottle, but if it is used, then at least eighty-five per cent of the grapes must come from that region.

American back labels are among the most prosaic (and, some might say, pretentious) you'll find. But two items are common to all. First, the phrase "contains sulfites". Most wines are made with the help of sulphur dioxide, but this warning is for acute asthmatics and others with special respiratory problems.

Second, there's the government warning that women should not drink alcoholic beverages during pregnancy and that consumption of alcohol impairs the ability to drive a car or operate machinery, and may cause health problems. There is a move to counter this by promoting the health benefits of moderate wine drinking. In the future, bottles may show the message: "We encourage you to consult your family doctor about the health effects of wine consumption."

Ridge
Top-class producer

RIDGE 1997 CALIFORNIA MONTE BELLO®

Monte Bello
For Ridge, the name of the vineyard is more important than the grapes used – a small but growing trend among New World producers

85% CABERNET SAUVIGNON, 11% MERLOT, 4% PETIT VERDOT
GROWN, PRODUCED & BOTTLED BY RIDGE VINEYARDS
17100 MONTE BELLO ROAD, CUPERTINO, CA 95014
12.5% VOL.   PRODUCE OF U.S.A.   750 ML

85% Cabernet, 11% Merlot, etc.
The precise make-up of the wine. Ridge's back labels contain even more information about the wine

Beaux Frères
The producer. It's French for "brothers-in-law", and one of the brothers-in-law who own the winery is the famous wine critic Robert Parker

The Beaux Frères Vineyard
No bought-in grapes, in other words

Willamette Valley, Oregon – premier Pinot Noir country

Unfined and Unfiltered
The winemakers have tried to make the wine as naturally as possible. Don't be surprised if there is some sediment

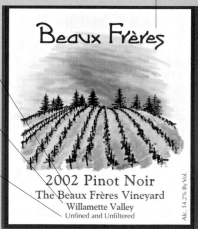

Beaux Frères

2002 Pinot Noir
The Beaux Frères Vineyard
Willamette Valley
Unfined and Unfiltered

Alc. 14.2% By Vol.

South America

While the bulk of the wines from Chile and Argentina are labelled according to grape variety, both countries have increasing numbers of prosaically named blended wines of top quality – with prices to match.

Chile

Although the range is expanding, Chile is still dominated by the big four varieties: Cabernet Sauvignon, Merlot, Chardonnay, and Sauvignon Blanc. When trying Sauvignon Blanc, keep in mind that it can be made from inferior Sauvignonasse, and that many "Merlots" contain Carmenère, an interesting but quite different grape. Regional specialties are recognized – Chardonnay and Sauvignon Blanc from Casablanca, Merlot from Colchagua, Cabernet Sauvignon from Maipo – but the producer's name is still the most important factor on a Chilean label.

Argentina

A wider variety of grapes are grown in Argentina. As well as the familiar French varieties, Spanish immigrants brought Tempranillo and (probably) the spicy Torrontés, while their Italian counterparts brought Nebbiolo, Sangiovese, Barbera, and Bonarda. The Mendoza region produces more than two-thirds of the country's wine, and probably a larger proportion of the exported wine. The region's higher western parts generally produce the best wines – look out for sub-zones such as Vistalba, Luján de Cuyo, and Tupungato.

Viña Casablanca (big letters)
The name of the producer – rather confusingly!

Valle de Casablanca (small letters)
The region

Sauvignon Blanc
Sauvignon Blanc, Chile's top white variety. Some Chilean Sauvignons still contain a proportion of the related but inferior Sauvignonasse

Fabre e Montmayou
French-inspired producer

Malbec
Argentina's trump-card grape

Luján de Cuyo Classy red wine district of Mendoza

Australia

If wine is now an easier drink for the world to enjoy, then the Aussies should take much credit for that. Quality has always been vitally important, of course, but user-friendly packaging counts a lot toward Australia's success, too. Easy-drinking wines with labels containing words that are easy to pronounce and easy to remember – it's a winning combination.

Many Australian wines are blends that are made up of grapes grown in different parts of the country, so you'll often find that two or more regions are mentioned on the label – Coonawarra/McLaren Vale, for example. Multi-regional blends often appear with a state designation, such as South Australia, or with the blanket South Eastern Australia label – which, in practice, means the grapes could come from anywhere outside Western Australia.

A wine industry body called the Geographical Indications Committee (GIC) is currently drawing up boundaries for Australian wine regions. The boundary divisions are based on variations in climate and also on geological differences. But there are no limits on the grape varieties that can be planted within these boundaries, nor on the quality and style of the wines produced there.

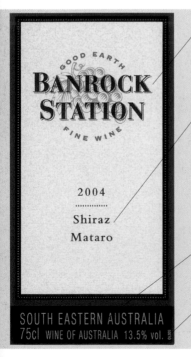

Banrock Station One of the many brands of BRL Hardy, now part of Constellation Wines, the world's largest wine company

Shiraz/Mataro Australia's most popular grape plus the revitalized Mataro, also known as Mourvèdre. The order of listing indicates that there will be at least as much (and probably more) Shiraz as Mataro

South Eastern Australia The appellation used for many a multi-regional blend. Quality ranges from basic to brilliant

13.5% Potent in European terms, typical for many New World wines

Chambers Rosewood Vineyards A top fortified wine producer

Rutherglen The region

Rare Muscat Muscats are now split into four categories. In ascending order of quality and richness they are: Rutherglen Muscat, Classic, Grand, and Rare

17.5% This is fortified wine, but it's not as alcoholic as many ports

New Zealand

There's far more to New Zealand wines than the words "Marlborough" and "Sauvignon Blanc". A country that was once dismissed as fit only for the lacklustre Müller-Thurgau is now producing world-class Pinot Noir, Chardonnay, and Riesling (and, of course, Sauvignon Blanc), as well as some very impressive Bordeaux-inspired blends. When it comes to the labels, there are few terms you'll encounter that are not self-explanatory.

In the same way that Australia uses the broad regional description of South Eastern Australia as a catch-all designation, so New Zealand has East Coast, an appellation that encompasses the following areas: Gisborne (also known as Poverty Bay), Hawke's Bay, and Wairarapa (also known as Martinborough) on the North Island; and Marlborough and Canterbury on the South Island. However, divisions are now starting to emerge within these main regions. In Hawke's Bay (which also appears as Hawkes Bay, depending on whose label you examine), the gravel-rich soils around Gimblett Road are proving to offer ideal conditions for red wine production. You may see a small gold sticker on the labels of some wines produced in that region, proclaiming that they are from the Gimblett Gravels.

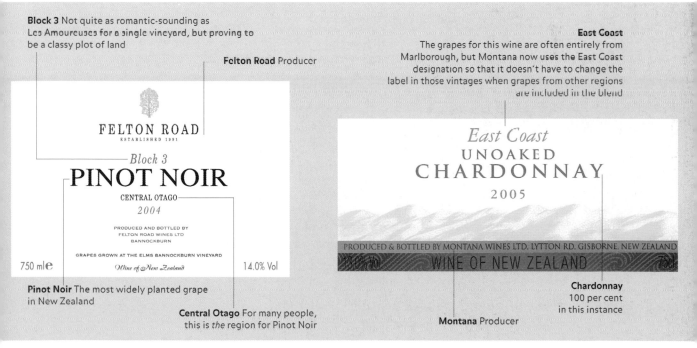

Block 3 Not quite as romantic-sounding as Les Amoureuses for a single vineyard, but proving to be a classy plot of land

Felton Road Producer

FELTON ROAD
ESTABLISHED 1991
Block 3
PINOT NOIR
CENTRAL OTAGO
2004
PRODUCED AND BOTTLED BY
FELTON ROAD WINES LTD
BANNOCKBURN
GRAPES GROWN AT THE ELMS BANNOCKBURN VINEYARD
Wine of New Zealand
750 ml℮   14.0% Vol

Pinot Noir The most widely planted grape in New Zealand

Central Otago For many people, this is *the* region for Pinot Noir

East Coast The grapes for this wine are often entirely from Marlborough, but Montana now uses the East Coast designation so that it doesn't have to change the label in those vintages when grapes from other regions are included in the blend

East Coast
UNOAKED
CHARDONNAY
2005
PRODUCED & BOTTLED BY MONTANA WINES LTD. LYTTON RD. GISBORNE. NEW ZEALAND
WINE OF NEW ZEALAND

Chardonnay 100 per cent in this instance

Montana Producer

South Africa

Those familiar with wines from other New World countries will have few problems with South African wines, but there are some terms that are unique to the Cape. The country's Wine of Origin (WO) appellation system divides the vineyards into regions, districts, and wards.

So the ward of Simonsberg-Stellenbosch lies in the district of Stellenbosch, which forms part of the Coastal Region. All the grapes must be from the stated area. There are also the more general appellations of Western Cape (often used when wines are blends from several WOs) and the rarely seen Northern Cape. Neither is a WO.

Sparkling wines made by the Champagne method go by the name of méthode cap classique (MCC), while Chenin Blanc – which is the Cape's most widely planted grape – is sometimes called Steen. The term "estate" also has an official meaning in South African wine law. Only wines made from grapes grown and vinified on the property in question can claim estate status.

Confirmation that a wine meets all these regulations appears in the form of a Wine and Spirit Board seal on the neck of the bottle. Only around a third of all South African wines are submitted for such certification. However, the majority of bottles that have been produced for export will be put forward for certification.

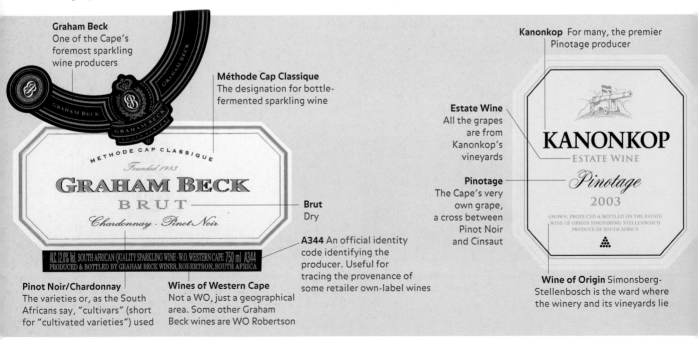

Graham Beck
One of the Cape's foremost sparkling wine producers

Méthode Cap Classique
The designation for bottle-fermented sparkling wine

Brut
Dry

A344 An official identity code identifying the producer. Useful for tracing the provenance of some retailer own-label wines

Pinot Noir/Chardonnay
The varieties or, as the South Africans say, "cultivars" (short for "cultivated varieties") used

Wines of Western Cape
Not a WO, just a geographical area. Some other Graham Beck wines are WO Robertson

Kanonkop For many, the premier Pinotage producer

Estate Wine
All the grapes are from Kanonkop's vineyards

Pinotage
The Cape's very own grape, a cross between Pinot Noir and Cinsaut

Wine of Origin Simonsberg-Stellenbosch is the ward where the winery and its vineyards lie

The rise of the gimmick label

"Real emetic fans will also go for a 'Hobart Muddy', and a prize-winning 'Cuiver Reserve Château Bottled Nuits St Wagga Wagga', which has a bouquet like an aborigine's armpit." The Monty Python Australian wine sketch might have seemed far-fetched back in the 1970s; however, today's shelves hold wines whose names aren't that far removed from "Château Chunder".

For instance, there's Marilyn Merlot from Napa Valley, with a different picture of Norma Jean for each vintage. There's a New Zealand Sauvignon Blanc called Cat's Pee on a Gooseberry Bush – that's the classic tasting note, after all. A pair of wines from the Californian producer Topolos are called Stu Pedasso and Rae Jean Beach (say them quickly to get the full effect). From southern France, there's a similar pair called Old Git and Old Tart. Gimmicks? Maybe, but those who have seen such wines won't forget them.

And they're no more of a gimmick than wines using the name of various creeks, peaks, ridges, and bridges. Even if these places exist, they often have little geographical connection to the wine. There is a Jacob's Creek in Australia's Barossa Valley, but most of the wine with that name is from a totally different region. King of the quirky label is Randall Grahm of Bonny Doon Vineyards, California. It can be hard to fully understand the allusions, but the wines have entertaining packaging. Where Grahm scores is that his wines are as interesting as his labels.

Bonny Doon Old Telegram Randall Grahm's Mataro alludes to Domaine du Vieux-Télégraphe in Châteauneuf-du-Pape. Grahm also has a Châteauneuf-styled wine called Le Cigare Volant (literally "The Flying Cigar"; the French equivalent of "flying saucer" or UFO), so called because the local council in Châteauneuf once issued a decree banning flying saucers from landing in the vineyards

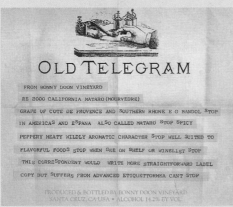

Fairview Goat-Roti
Charles Back's winery in Paarl is home to both goats and vines – the estate is also a major producer of cheese. The goat theme continues with Goats do Roam and Goat d'Afrique. Sadly, some producers in France's Rhône Valley fail to be impressed by Back's labels, and have started legal action – although nothing has yet been resolved

THE TASTE OF WINE

It's important to start tasting wine like a professional, discovering the various aromas, flavours, and textures that are unique to each one, and learning to appreciate which styles of wine you like best — and which you don't. Here's how to get the most out of each and every bottle you open, and some information about the factors that influence the liquid in your glass.

Why do we "taste" wine?

Now that you've got plenty of information on choosing, buying, serving, and storing wine, the time has come to get stuck in and taste the stuff. But why is it so important to "taste" wine when you could just knock it back?

Put simply, the more you think about the flavours, aromas, and textures of wine, the more you will get out of it. If you simply swallow a mouthful without savouring its complexity, you will miss out on a great deal. Once you spend some time examining its aroma, fruitiness, richness, and finish, an awful lot more about an individual bottle is revealed. No one wants to sip wine in a serious manner at parties, but those who get used to doing some "proper" wine tasting from time to time find that they even start to enjoy a sociable glass much more. That's because they gradually build up a framework of reference that they keep developing, constantly comparing and contrasting each different style. The more you try new wines, and the more you think about the characteristics of each one, the more you will become captivated by the subject of wine.

And, of course, the more you will be able to rule out the duds. Wine tasting isn't just about discovering exciting, brilliant new flavours; it's also about finding out what you *don't* like. That might be because a bottle is faulty (*see* page 79), or because it doesn't match a particular dish, or because it just isn't for you. But to learn more about what you do and don't like, you need to concentrate on tasting wine like a professional.

The first step is to look carefully at your wine; its colour and viscosity can tell you quite a lot about the liquid in your glass. Then concentrate on the aroma, swirling vigorously to release the bouquet. Next up is a real taste, so take a sip and think about flavour and texture. Tasting wine is not just about spotting fruity flavours, of course, so think hard about levels of acidity, tannins, oak, sweetness, and so on. Ask yourself whether the wine has good overall balance, and, of course, whether you actually like it (desirability is an elusive quality; only you can say if you want to drink it or not).

On the next few pages there are more details on how to taste wine and what to look for, as well that guide to spotting faulty bottles. Good luck!

Sight

"Looking" is probably the bit of wine tasting that we tend to dismiss as we reach for a glass without thinking. But a wine's appearance is part of its appeal, so take some time to examine the colour and clarity of the liquid you are about to drink.

It helps to hold the glass against a white background. Tip reds slightly at an angle, too, and look at the edge of the liquid to assess the colour. So what are we looking for? If it's a sparkling wine, ideally you'll see streams and streams of bubbles, preferably fine, small ones, as these taste more crisp and refined on the tongue than big ones.

White and sparkling wines

For both sparkling and white wines, the colour varies considerably, from extremely pale with a slight hint of green through to a brighter straw colour and even a rich, bright gold. Generally speaking, the paler wines tend to be lighter, drier, unoaked styles, while a richer colour indicates possible sweetness, ripeness, and/or oakiness.

Older wines are often richer in colour. Check for the clarity of white wines, too – they should be bright and completely clear – not cloudy. Finally, do look at the texture of the liquid as you swirl it round the glass. Some whites are thinner and more watery than others. That's not necessarily a bad thing, but it is an indication of style. Richer, more powerful, or sweeter whites look more viscous and "gloopy" when you swirl them, sometimes leaving rich trails of liquid down the sides of the glass. Sweet wines will be particularly weighty and rich in appearance.

Red wines

With reds, the appearance can give some clues about the age and style of the wine. Look at the rim and ascertain whether the colour is deep red or light (a sign of whether the wine is rich or not), and whether the red colour is a purple-bluey red (which indicates youth) or a brick-browny red (which indicates age). Swirl the glass around and you may get a sense of how rich, powerful,and heavily extracted the wine is – or not. Light reds will literally look lighter, thinner, and less dense in colour.

Nose

Try an experiment at home. Pour a glass of wine one-third full, then sniff it quickly without swirling the liquid. Now try again, but this time swirl it hard and take a series of big sniffs. You should notice a huge difference as the aroma is released.

What you've done is "swoosh" the wine around in contact with the air and opened it out, literally sending some molecules up into your nostrils. The aroma should be revealed much more clearly, and in a good wine this will add a great deal to its overall appeal. The smell of a wine is crucially important to your enjoyment, so do swirl, sniff, and make the most of it!

What's in a whiff?

First of all, assess the freshness of the wine. This is when you may pick up a mustiness if the wine is "corked" (*see* page 79). So before going any farther, have a sniff for sheer crispness, fruitiness, and general appeal. The initial impression should tell you whether you have an aromatic wine or one with a more neutral perfume. Then sniff again, this time looking for particular characteristics. If it's a sparkling wine, note any yeasty, biscuity character. If it's a dry white, perhaps some grassiness or herbaceousness will be lurking in there with the fruit. Look out for oakiness in both reds and whites – a creamy vanilla or wood-spice aroma is a give-away.

As for fruit character, expect tropical scents from rich New World Chardonnays and Viogniers, ripe gooseberry from modern, new-wave Sauvignon Blancs, but more lemony, appley aromas from cool-climate Sauvignon Blancs and Rieslings. Reds made from Pinot Noir and Gamay (Beaujolais) tend to have an aroma of summer-pudding fruits (strawberries and cherries), but watch for red plums in Merlot, cassis in Cabernet Sauvignon, and peppery, toffee hints in Syrah/Shiraz.

Wines noted for their highly aromatic qualities include Gewurztraminers; Muscats; New Zealand Sauvignon Blancs; older Rieslings; mellow, oaky red Riojas; peppery Rhône reds; and fresh, cherryish rosés. Some wines, such as light Italian whites, don't have much aroma, but that will be fine if the wine still tastes fresh and good.

Taste

Of course, the flavour of a wine is its most important asset, so get as much as you can out of it. Slosh the wine around your mouth to get it into every corner and think about the "finish" as well.

Don't glug your wine; sip it slowly and savour its flavour, not to mention its texture. Just as you swirled the wine to release its aroma, you now need to open up the flavour of the liquid. To do this, take a sip of wine, keeping it at the front of the mouth, then pull a bit of air into and over it (don't worry about the slurping noise – wine tasting isn't supposed to be genteel!). This aerates the wine and releases the flavours. Slosh the wine around your mouth, too, so the different parts of your tongue can assess sweetness, acidity, sourness, and so on.

Do think about the obvious fruit flavours (there's more on this subject on page 76), but don't forget all the other aspects of a wine's flavour. First and foremost, does it taste good? This might sound trite, but really a wine needs to be appealing more than anything else. Work out if you like it, and if you would want to drink much of it. Sometimes a wine has bags of flavour, structure, tannin, sweetness, etc., which might impress you on first taste, but that doesn't necessarily mean it is "moreish". Be especially careful not to overlook a subtle, elegant style of wine. Ask yourself if you would want to sit down with a bottle of it and actually consume it or not.

A question of balance

As you taste the wine, think, too, about the overall balance. Acidity adds freshness (see page 73); oak might enhance the wine; sweetness might be prominent. Ask yourself if all these factors are well balanced – does the sum of these parts actually work? Sometimes a wine is simply too acidic, or too tannic, or too sweet/dry.

Now try to capture those fruity flavours – which fruits exactly? What other flavours have you noticed? Cream, pepper, oak, honey, grass... Look for unusual flavours as well.

The finish

The finish is a very important part of the tasting process. Assessing the finish comes after you swallow or spit out the wine. It's the impression you are left with.

Some characteristics of this amazing liquid shine out at the end, rather than when you first put the wine in your mouth. Sweetness, for example, tends to show up in the finish, as does high acidity, which makes your tongue tingle and your mouth water. Heavy tannins make the end of the flavour seem furry and dry (*see* page 75).

Some wines have a big finish, with concentrated flavours that seem to go on and on after you've swallowed, while others fall flat, and seem dull and flavourless at the end (these are referred to as having a "short" finish). Think, too, about how young/old the wine is, and whether it has more life ahead of it, or if it is starting to show signs of tiredness.

Points to consider

Before you move onto the next wine, think again about *if* you would like to drink this one; *when* you would most desire it (cold weather/hot weather/everyday drinking/special occasion...); and *how* you match it with food (which dishes would work best, or is it an apéritif style?). Then ask yourself if it is good value for money.

Always compare and contrast a new wine with the others you have tasted recently. Comparison is essential for building up a good idea of what's out there. For example, ask yourself whether this wine is richer or lighter than wines X and Y; is it more powerful and spicy than the other big reds you tried last week; is it a better example of the same grape variety you have enjoyed from a different part of the world? Answer questions like these and take note of whether you actually drink the wine later on that evening – a very good sign of a desirable bottle, of course! Anything that you are not inspired to drink isn't worth buying in the future.

Acidity

Who wants their wine to taste acidic? It sounds off-putting, but the right levels of acidity are essential in order for a wine to taste fresh, vibrant, and mouth-watering.

In fact, without enough acid, a wine can taste flat, dull, and lacking in freshness. A sweet wine with low acidity seems cloying; a rich red without enough seems heavy and plodding. And don't even think about drinking a rosé, dry sherry, or sparkling wine that doesn't have a crisp, tongue-tingling dose of tart acid.

Fresh acidity helps a wine to go well with food; the tangy, clean character cuts through any fattiness. Acidity also acts as a preservative, so good levels are crucial. A high-acid wine might well keep for years; fine Rieslings and Loire Chenin Blancs are good examples of this.

Of course, the amount of acidity in a wine varies considerably. It depends on several factors: the grape variety, the time of the harvest, how much the grapes have been exposed to the sun, and the climate in the region where the fruit was grown.

Acidity and climate

In hot areas, grapes can ripen without retaining enough acidity. Here the grower might choose to pick early, or might add acid in the winery (this is illegal in most of Europe, but not in the New World) – *see* page 77. Grapes grown in cool areas (think Germany, France's Loire Valley, Champagne...) have higher levels of acidity. Sometimes the fruit is too acidic. This might be corrected by using calcium carbonate, or by putting the wine through a process known as malolactic fermentation, which turns the malic acid present in the wine into softer-tasting lactic acid.

Red wines tend to be put through malolactic fermentation, and increasingly it is used for softer, richer styles of white, especially Chardonnays. You can often tell that a Chardonnay has been through this process because it has a creamier, richer, more buttery character than usual. It's not necessarily a better wine – just a different style.

Alcohol, ripeness, & sweetness

Don't make the mistake of thinking alcohol levels are the same for all table wines – they vary considerably and it is worth knowing why. Alcohol levels and sugar levels are inextricably linked, so here's more on sweetness, too.

Yeast converts the natural sugars in wine into alcohol. Simple. The riper and sweeter the grapes, the more alcohol can be produced, so wines from hotter regions tend to be more alcoholic than those from cooler climates. The richest reds from the New World can reach over 15% ABV (alcohol by volume), while the lightest whites from cooler spots, such as the Mosel in Germany, weigh in at only around 8% ABV. This huge difference can be detected not only by the rate at which you feel drunk, but also in the taste of the wine. Powerful, richly alcoholic wines taste bigger, more weighty, and viscous than light, thinner, low-alcohol wines.

How sweet wines are made

Sweet wines are made in several ways. If the yeast has stopped fermenting naturally before all the sugar has been converted to alcohol, then residual sweetness is left in the finished wine. Sometimes the fermentation is deliberately halted before it has finished. This is done by adding spirit in the case of sweet fortified wines such as port, or by chilling the fermenting juice and extracting the yeast. In the case of some sweet wines, the grapes are left on the vine until they overripen and shrivel, producing concentrated, sweet juice to work with, or else they are picked after botrytis (noble rot) has attacked them, shrivelling them again. In certain areas, a process called chaptalization is used, where sugar is added to the fermenting vat. This is allowed in Germany, parts of France, and other pockets of Europe.

So how do winemakers in cool-climate regions ripen their grapes properly? They should plant in the warm microclimates that they have, and choose grape varieties that ripen more easily without great heat. Some cut back the leafy vines, exposing the fruit to the sun more fully. There are fewer unripe wines around than a generation ago, as growers and winemakers have mastered the art of ripening grapes more fully.

Tannin

Just like acidity, tannin — the substance that gives a rich red wine its almost furry, chewy texture, structure, and dry finish — doesn't actually sound very nice. Yet it is essential to the character of many wines.

And it's why some full-bodied wines stand up so well to hearty food. Admittedly, a very tannic young red is difficult to assess on its own, but you have to imagine that you are going to eat a rare steak or a chunk of hard, mature cheese with it. The protein in this kind of meal marries perfectly with the tannins, and the wine will taste softer and more appealing in this context. That said, some wines are over-tannic and mouth-puckering when young, even with food. If they are premium reds with lots of fruit and acidity to balance the tannins (in other words, simply a very powerful, immature fine wine), they usually benefit from ageing for several years, during which time the tannins soften and mellow.

Tannins are a group of organic chemicals found in the seeds, stems, and skins of grapes. The tannins in seeds can be bitter, which is why winemakers take care not to crush them in the winery. Stems are sometimes used and sometimes removed – a decision for the winemaker each time the process starts again, depending on the style of wine he/she wants. The main source of desirable tannins, though, is the grape skin. Small, thick-skinned grapes give up more tannin than large, thin-skinned ones. And the winemaker will decide how hard to press or crush the skins according to how much tannin (and colour) he/she wants to extract. Riper grapes produce fewer harsh tannins than unripe ones. Now and again in New World countries, tannin is added in the winery if the very ripe grapes naturally have too little.

Expect to find tannic reds from Bordeaux (young, Cabernet-rich blends); Italy (the toughest, most serious young Piedmontese and Tuscan reds); the northern Rhône and southern France; California (premium Cabernet Sauvignons and Zinfandels); South Africa and Australia (Cabernet Sauvignons and Cabernet blends in particular). If you dislike tannic wines, choose silky-smooth Pinot Noir or even easygoing, soft Gamay.

To mellow and soften a tannic wine, aerate it by swirling the wine around a large glass, or by decanting the entire bottle. For more on decanting, *see* pages 32–3.

Fruit

Isn't it strange how wine so rarely tastes of grapes? Instead, some red varieties produce black-fruit flavours of cassis and blackberries, while others are redolent of strawberries and cherries. White wines often taste of gooseberries, lemons, and apples.

The hyperbolic way in which wine is described is sometimes referred to as the "fruit salad" school of wine writing. While certain descriptions do indeed go over the top, it is hard to argue that wines *don't* smell and taste of different fruits. Each vine has, after all, evolved over centuries to take on particular characteristics, so its flavours may have become exaggerated in the same way as the features of some pedigree dogs. Use of specific clones of grape varieties helps the modern grower pin down even more specific, distinctive traits.

The fruit character depends to a large extent on where it is grown. Hence a cool-climate Chardonnay tends to have a more citrus-fruit and apple flavour, while a hot-climate one heads into tropical fruit: peaches, pineapples, mangoes. Riesling from a cool spot in Germany is all lemon, green apple, and white blossom, while a richer Australian example has much more lime juiciness to the fore. And Sauvignon Blanc that seems so minerally, lemony, and bone-dry in the Loire gives us an explosion of gooseberry, tomato leaf, and asparagus in New Zealand.

When tasting wine, think not only about the obvious fruit character, but around the subject, too. So if you spot "oranges" in a wine, for example, expand on it. Are they ripe oranges or clementines, or perhaps preserved oranges, or dried orange peel, or an orange with cloves stuck in it? You can let yourself go over this one. Likewise, the cassis commonly associated with Cabernet Sauvignon might be blackcurrant jam, or spiced blackcurrants, or ones with a minty edge, or the blackcurrant of a fruit gum.

If the whole thing is getting up your nose (literally) and you crave a wine that actually smells and tastes of grapes, then try a dry Muscat. It has the same fragrance and flavour as crunching on a fresh, chilled bunch of green table grapes – very refreshing, in more ways than one!

Other ingredients

So what else is in your bottle of wine apart from fermented grapes (assuming this is not Uncle Joe's turnip-top "wine", that is)? It's worth looking at the "MOG": Matter Other than Grapes, as the Aussies call it...

...which makes it sound as though all manner of bugs, snakes, and bird droppings make it into the crushers. There may be a *tiny* bit of this, but MOG really refers to the additives such as tannin, sugar, acidity, preservatives, and fining (clarification) agents that go into certain wines.

Tannin (*see* page 75) can be added to wines that lack grip and body; it is produced commercially from pressed grape skins specially for this purpose. Tartaric, citric, or ascorbic acid is sometimes added to very ripe wines (usually from hot-climate regions) which are perceived as lacking that crisp, mouth-watering quality. Sulphur dioxide can be added as a cleaning agent to kill off bacteria and unwanted yeasts, and as a preservative against oxidation (just as it used to preserve dried fruits, for example). Too much sulphur, and you'll notice a chemical pong to your wine – more about this on page 79 and in the Wine & Health section on page 150.

Clearing & fining agents

Natural bentonite clay is used to absorb any solid matter such as mouldy bits or the odd stray piece of grape stalk or skin. It's poured in, allowed to pick up any stray solids, and then completely removed from the liquid, taking all the unwanted bits with it. Fining agents are also used sometimes to rush the clarification process – in other words, to help clear the liquid of any solid matter without waiting for everything to fall to the bottom of the vat.

Fining agents include gelatin, casein (from milk), egg white, and isinglass (from fish). This may alarm vegetarians and vegans, but bear in mind that they are usually used in minute quantities – egg whites at only two parts per million, for example – and a negligible amount remains in the finished wines. They also do the job more delicately than machines such as centrifuges. But if you object to animal products being used at all, then look out for some wines which are labelled "suitable for vegetarians/vegans", which means this type of fining agent has not been used.

Organic & biodynamic wine

Organic wine is growing in popularity, along with all organic food and drink. So just what does it mean when a wine is labelled "organic"? And does it taste any better than "ordinary" wine?

There are plenty of myths surrounding organic wine: one is that it isn't made from grapes at all, but from different fruits (it's not), or that it comes from different varieties of grape (nope). The simple fact is that organic wine is made from organically grown grapes and produced according to strict regulations in the winery. The vines are free from pesticides, fungicides, herbicides, and artificial fertilizers, while the wine itself is free from all artificial preservatives and uses as little of any kind of preservative as possible.

Truth is, many wines have been organic for centuries, but their makers don't choose to trumpet the fact. Many other wineries have converted to organic viticulture in recent years as they have seen the popularity of these products grow, and they have also realized that the natural methods of production are much kinder on their land in the long term.

It can be tough on the producer, though. It takes years to achieve organic status, and if a damp, diseased vintage means one recourse to spraying with unapproved substances, that status is easily lost again. Obviously, it is simpler to turn organic in dry, sunny conditions than it is in damp, cooler ones. But wherever it is attempted, growing grapes organically is labour-intensive, which means it's more expensive, too – so expect organic wines to cost a little more than their non-organic equivalents.

So does the wine taste better? Not really. There are poor and great organic wines, just as there are non-organic ones, but overall organic vineyards receive more tender loving care than others, and they can produce healthier vines. You might just be able to spot a "truer" flavour – a more Chardonnay-ish Chardonnay, so to speak. In the main though, it just feels good to know that the soil, vines, and natural wildlife of the vineyard are thriving much more under organic practices. (*See* Wine and Health on page 150 for more on organic wine and allergies.)

Much has been made of biodynamic viticulture in the twenty-first century. This is a more extreme version of organics – like a vegan version of vegetarianism. A biodynamic producer uses organic principles but also follows planetary and lunar cycles to plot the stages of pruning, harvesting, etc., throughout the year. Somewhat New Age methods are also employed in the vineyard, such as burying cows' horns filled with special preparations among the vines. The results, it has to be said, are impressive: many biodynamic wines taste exceptionally pure and clean. But how much this is due to the methods, and how much to a huge amount of hands-on tending of the vines is hard to tell.

Faults in wine

When is a wine faulty? Here's a quick guide to the problems found in some bottles, and what to do if you end up with one.

Don't be intimidated by what seems like a mysterious subject. Quite simply, if a wine smells and/or tastes musty, vinegary, or oxidized (about which more in a minute) or if it has a foreign object in it, take it back and complain. Whether you are in a shop or a restaurant, you should receive a replacement bottle and no quibbling. That said, no one can expect a replacement bottle if a) the first one has been drained or b) if you simply didn't like a perfectly acceptable example of a valid style of wine. If it was merely too dry or too sweet, too rich or too light, that's just bad luck – buy something different next time. A faulty bottle should fall into one of the following categories:

"Corked" wine

Cork taint is a continuing problem, affecting as many as one in fifteen bottles that have a natural cork, by our estimate. It has nothing to do with a crumbly cork, which leaves unsightly pieces in the wine but doesn't spoil the flavour. Corked wine has been affected by a mould on the natural bark stopper which has given the liquid a musty, dank, cardboardy character. Imagine damp old kitchen cloths in the case of a badly corked wine. However, some wines are only mildly corked, which just makes them taste disappointingly flat and fruitless. Leave a suspect bottle open to air for a while and any cork taint will get worse. Choose screwcaps or plastic stoppers for a cork-free experience.

Oxidized wine

This is where the air has got in and spoiled the wine, leaving a strange, sherry-like character to the flavour (but nowhere near as nice as good sherry). The wine tastes "off", in the same way as a brown piece of apple tastes off.

Over-sulphured wine

Sulphur dioxide is used as a preservative (*see* pages 77 and 157), but occasionally the "struck match" smell of it is quite off-putting. A light smell of sulphur should dissipate if you swirl your glass vigorously, but do return heavily sulphured wines. If the idea of sulphur bothers you, stick to organic wine, which is made using less sulphur or none at all.

Foreign bodies

Don't worry about sediment, which collects naturally in some bottles of rich red wine and port, and can be decanted off easily (*see* pages 32–3), or about harmless white crystals, which are flavourless tartrate deposits. Anything else you find in your bottle (including fruit flies) is grounds for demanding a replacement.

Terroir

How much does it matter *where* your grapes are grown? Can soil, climate, and so on make a great difference to the flavours in your glass? Read on...

The French have a word for it: "terroir" is an almost mystical concept that sums up a wine's sense of place. Not only the soil and climate, but also the rainfall, the gradient of the vineyard, even the cultural environment and winemaking traditions where the grapes were grown are considered deeply important to the finished wine in some parts of the world, mainly Europe.

That's why many premium European brands do not proclaim their grape varieties proudly on their labels. Instead, the place where the grapes were grown comes to the fore: Chablis, Sancerre, Mosel, Rioja, *et al.* are all thought to be far more important than the type of vine used. The idea is that, above all else, a wine bears and retains the distinctive character of the area where it was made. And no other wine (despite being made with the same grapes) can taste exactly like that.

The New World view

The approach of New World winemakers used to be quite different. The grapes and the winemakers were paramount here. The theory was that the vineyard was simply a scrap of soil, and a similar style could be replicated by using the same techniques and the same grapes in other sites. Now the two worlds have drawn a little closer together, with more European winemakers putting grape varieties more clearly on labels, while New World winemakers have realized the potential of individual styles of wine from particular regions or vineyards, and are placing more emphasis on terroir. (*See* also page 12.)

Most people today appreciate that *all* these factors are important. Of course terroir dictates a wine's style to a large extent, as it is the unique set of conditions under which an individual wine is made. Grape varieties are vital for many consumers today; weaned on New World single-varietal wines, we actively want to see the grapes displayed on the label. And winemakers are another piece in the jigsaw. Clearly it's no good having the perfect terroir if a clod-hopping *vigneron* is at work in the winery!

Winemaking decisions in the vineyard

Although much of what goes on in a vineyard is decided by Mother Nature, the grower has many crucial decisions to make, and these affect the character of the finished wine. Time, then, to learn about some of the work that takes place on the vines.

The good grower, of course, selects a plot carefully. Ideally, the soils are poor and not hugely fertile, as that helps to keep the crop low, producing small amounts of highly flavoured grapes. The soil should also be well drained. Irrigation might be needed in arid areas, and the type of water supply (slow drip-feed or flood irrigation) is a subject of hot debate.

Training & pruning

The trellis (wire-training system) counts for much, too. Some trellises are deliberately set up to separate the canopy of the vine in order to expose the grapes to the sun more than usual; others take the vine high up off the ground away from dampness and rot. Certain vines are not trained on wires but are left to grow in bushes close to the soil; this happens in very hot, dry climates as the bush shape helps retain moisture. The skill lies in selecting the type of trellis to suit the climate/grape variety/style of wine required.

Pruning is another important task. The shoots of the vine are cut back in the spring to stop the vine growing too many leaves, and some of the developing bunches of grapes might be taken off later in the season to reduce the harvest and help keep the flavours of the remaining bunches concentrated. Sometimes the canopy of leaves around each ripening bunch is cut back to let the hot sun in.

Harvesting methods

As for harvesting, much is done by machine these days. These machines are sometimes set to work by night, especially in very warm climates, bringing in the grapes while they are cool, which helps keep them fresh. Hand-picking is usually done in places where it is simply too difficult to use machines. Steeply terraced vineyards are often hand-harvested. The other time when picking by hand is necessary is when careful selection of bunches is required – for example, when botrytis-affected grapes are taken off to be made into sweet wines.

Winemaking decisions in the winery

So the harvest is in, and the winemaker can start work. Although the fermentation process is a natural one, there are still plenty of decisions to be made that determine what the finished wine will taste like.

Some winemakers are highly interventionist, imposing much on a wine such as different yeast strains, heavy use of oak-ageing, and tinkering with sugar, tannin, and/or acidity. Others prefer more natural methods – letting the grapes speak for themselves, as they would call it.

Today, however, one thing everyone is sure about is hygiene. A decent winery should be kept scrupulously clean, preferably with spotless stainless-steel tanks for fermentation and regular hosing down of the winery floors and walls. Some winemakers have stuck with open-top fermenters for rich reds in particular, but they clean them an awful lot more than they used to just one generation ago. This emphasis on cleanliness is one of the reasons that wines taste much fresher today than they did in the past.

Temperature control is another important step forward that caught on in the late twentieth century. Keeping the grape must cool is vital if you are to keep the fresh, crisp flavours in the finished wine, and this is especially important for white and pink wines. Many stainless-steel tanks now have refrigeration systems built into them, which winemakers use to control the temperature of the liquid they are working on.

Using yeast

Winemakers can also choose whether to use natural yeasts or to add a cultivated strain. Laboratory-produced yeast strains give a consistent character to the finished wine – in other words, the winemaker can know fairly precisely what effect the yeast will have. But others feel wild yeast gives a more "natural", authentic, and, some would say, complex flavour to the wine.

And finally, you should know that very few wines these days are made with foot-trodden grapes. Rather sadly, feet have been replaced by myriad high-tech mechanical presses, some of which squash the fruit gently, while others just give it a good old crush. The winemaker can choose the type of press to suit the style of wine wanted – which makes feet more or less redundant!

Oak

Of all the winemaker's decisions, those that relate to oak are among the most crucial. Used carefully, fermentation and ageing in oak barrels can enhance a wine no end – but it can be overdone.

It's like any addition to the cooking pot: salt, pepper, chilli, and other spices. A little can be used to round out the other flavours and complement them, but too much and it starts to overwhelm the whole dish. In the 1980s and 1990s, too much oak was used on some wines, giving the finished product a wooden, resinous flavour that put some people off Chardonnay in particular for good.

It's a shame oak got a bad reputation in some quarters, as judicious oak-ageing can really add something special: a hint of complexity and warmth, a touch of creamy, spicy, toasty character without obscuring the fruit flavours. Indeed, many of the world's top wines – reds and whites – are aged in oak. Fine clarets, top white Burgundies, red Rioja, and serious New World wines are often aged in 225-litre barriques from France or America (American oak imparts a fuller, creamier, more vanilla character than French).

Winemakers can choose how long to keep the wine in barrel, and how old the casks are; younger barrels provide more oak influence than older ones. But oak casks are expensive, and some winemakers resort to using separated staves instead. The staves are plunged into fermentation or storage tanks to add an oaky character. The use of wood chips is even cheaper. The chips are dunked into the storage tank and left there until the required flavour has leached out – a bit like a huge tea bag soaking in the pot. Barriques are reckoned to give the most refined flavour, while staves are a decent second-best; chips can produce a rather more crude, even bitter result.

Don't close your mind (or taste-buds) to oak. Many people declare that they dislike oaked whites in particular, but try an elegant Chablis (say, one which has had just a proportion of the wine aged briefly in oak before blending) and you may enjoy the very light, subtle dab of oak. Bear in mind that oakier whites are very good partners for rich food – better, often, than unoaked whites.

It might also help to know that some Champagnes and dessert wines are aged in oak, and they never seem to taste overtly oaky. If we haven't convinced you and you really want to avoid oaky whites, though, go for Riesling, Gewurztraminer, Sauvignon Blanc (apart from the Fumé Blanc style, which is oaky), or a top-end Pinot Grigio. Wines like these are rarely, if ever, oaked, and focus on crisp, aromatic, fresh-fruit character.

Personal taste

Finally, when tasting, learn to trust your own instincts about wine. Sampling wine and discovering what you like (and don't like) is highly individual – as much so as developing a sense of what you like to read or cook. Make sure no one tells you what you *should* enjoy.

Don't be bothered if your partner or best mate doesn't like your favourite wine. There are no "rights" and "wrongs" when it comes to an individual taste in the stuff. For example, some people simply loathe medium-sweet white wines, finding them cloying and sickly, while others adore them, relishing the riper, softer, more honeyed flavours than those found in bone-dry styles. That's fine. And if you swear the Syrah you are tasting has a distinct note of black treacle while your friend finds nothing but blackberries, then that's fine, too. Keep your own tasting notes (or memories) and use them to choose the wines that suit *you*.

But do keep an open mind. It's a real mistake to dismiss a whole area of wine, as in "I hate Chardonnay," or "I hate Australian wine," or "I hate sherry." There are zillions of different Chardonnays, many tasting quite different from each other. Australia is a huge country, making an amazingly diverse selection of wine styles, and as for sherry, well, if you still associate it only with great-auntie's sweet cream from Cyprus, then you are seriously out of touch. So while not everything is for everyone, do bear in mind the sheer range out there, and approach each tasting prepared to be wowed. It's vitally important to try as many varied styles of wine as you can if you want to keep finding new flavours, aromas, and textures. Don't get stuck in a rut.

Moving on
Make yourself try new wines at every opportunity. If a wine shop is holding a tasting, or simply has some bottles open to try, then get stuck in (you can always spit out if driving...). At a drinks party, sample small glasses of two or three different wines instead of sticking to one. Look into the nooks and crannies of the shop shelves for interesting new bottles and don't just buy the big brands on special offer – more exciting, tasty stuff is out there!

How to set up a tasting

It's interesting and instructive to practise wine tasting at home on your own, but how much more fun to do it in a group, when you can compare and contrast your reactions to different styles (and share the cost). Here are some tips on throwing a wine tasting.

- Consider setting a theme for the evening, as a large tasting of disparate styles and price points can be confusing. So, for example, choose to taste wines from one region, or one grape variety (and its blends), or go for wines that all cost around the same. You might decide to look at "wines for the summer months" or "wines to go with Christmas lunch". Get everyone to bring a bottle.

- Decide whether to have a blind tasting. This means the labels are covered up (with foil or plastic bags) so tasters can't bring any preconceptions to bear on the bottles they try. The labels, along with the prices, are revealed only when everyone has sampled the wine and decided on their verdicts. Blind tastings are a great way of discovering that you do, in fact, like Riesling, or you do think claret is overpriced, and so on.

- Provide spittoons/jugs for dumping leftovers, plus napkins, and plain crackers and mineral water to clear the palate. Try to avoid serving any canapés or other nibbles while tasting, as it is distracting for the taste-buds. Taste the lightest, driest wines first, moving on through to the richest/sweetest styles – it's easier on the palate.

- Make notes. It's not obligatory, of course, but a tasting note, however brief, helps you remember the wines you liked best, even months later. No one else has to be privy to your personal tasting notes, so write away to your heart's content, using abbreviations if you are scribbling quickly. You might even consider ranking the wines, or giving them points out of twenty or 100.

- Eat well afterwards. No one wants to go home from a wine tasting with a grumbling empty stomach. Sampling wine makes one hungry, so why not continue the theme of the evening with food that comes from the same region as the wines, or dishes that suit the season, or even ones that come at a similar price point?

GRAPE VARIETIES

Grapes are just grapes, right? Different varieties of vine can't make that much difference to how a wine tastes, surely? Wrong. The particular grape varieties that go into your bottle are crucial to determining the character of your wine. So here is an introduction to the most important grapes – and some of the more obscure ones, too – from white to red.

Chardonnay

It's grown all over the world, and our shop shelves are stuffed with it. Some adore it; others claim to be bored with Chardonnay, especially the richly oaky, toasty, super-ripe styles. But don't give up on this grape, as there are plenty of other sides to its personality.

Character

This depends on where it's grown and how the winemaker has chosen to craft it. It is a malleable grape that thrives in many climates and takes well to oak maturation. Chardonnay tends to be generously fruity (peaches, ripe apples, oranges, pineapples), but that fruitiness can be transformed into relatively lean, crisp, and unoaked flavours or rendered heavily wooded, toasty, and vanilla-rich. It's one of the three Champagne grapes, and is also used for other sparklers around the world. Still Chardonnay is usually unblended, but it does make a cheapish, cheerful duo with Semillon in Australia. Successful in most winemaking countries of the world, top examples come from Burgundy (white Burgundy is almost always 100 per cent Chardonnay), and there are those who swear that bottles labelled Chablis, Meursault, Puligny-Montrachet, and so on are among the best white wines in the world (fewer claims are made for Burgundy's cheapest offerings). Look out for Chardonnay from California, Chile, Argentina, New Zealand, Australia, South Africa, Italy, Spain, France's Languedoc and Limoux regions, Austria, eastern Europe, Long Island (USA)... just about everywhere, in other words. There are even decent Chardonnays springing up from Greece and Canada.

When to drink it

Enjoy the crispest unoaked wines on their own or with simple fish and seafood dishes; lightly oaked Chardonnays with creamy pasta or fish in butter/cream sauces or luxury seafood like lobster; and the richest, oaked Chardonnays with roast poultry and smoked salmon. Semillon/Chardonnay is good with mild chicken or prawn curries. For more on food and wine matching *see* pages 132–49.

Future bets

Has been hugely popular and fashionable of late, and is now suffering from an "overkill" effect in some quarters. Tends to be perceived unfairly as a beginner's wine, although real connoisseurs will always appreciate its versatility and the complexity of its best examples.

Chenin Blanc

Rather underrated except by Loire Valley wine buffs, Chenin Blanc can make complex, long-lived, dry, medium, and sweet white wines. France and South Africa are the most important areas where good and great wine is created, but do avoid the very cheapest Chenins.

Character

Pick a poor Chenin Blanc and you can expect little character. What there is can taste rather sour and/or musty, with an aroma sometimes described as "wet wool". But persevere: a good Chenin is lively and fresh, with apple, quince, and lime notes and sometimes a dab of honey, even a rich, beeswax texture in the more serious wines. Some are bone-dry and very sharp when young; this style needs plenty of time in the cellar to evolve and soften. Others are off-dry, with a tempting, baked-apple flavour and perhaps a hint of walnut, and there are some luscious but very fresh dessert wines, too. Sparklers in the Loire are also made from this grape. Little is grown outside France and South Africa. It's rarely oaked. Don't look for the grape on French bottles, but choose by place-name; the cool Loire Valley is the region to look out for, and the best wines of all tend to be Savennières (bone-dry), premium Vouvray (often off-dry), Saumur (sparkling), Bonnezeaux, and Coteaux du Layon (sweet). Cheaper examples, like Anjou Blanc, can be dull and disappointing. South Africa is the other major source for Chenin Blanc – expect Cape Chenins to be fruity, limey, fairly straightforward crowd-pleasers, although the occasional more complex, rich, and sometimes even oaky bottle pops up, too.

When to drink it

The lightest, driest still and sparkling Chenins make clean, refreshing apéritifs, while the good-value, easy-drinking Cape wines can provide tasty party whites. Premium-quality South Africans and dry/off-dry Loires should be paired with seafood or fish, or try medium examples with pork and apple sauce, or cold ham and cheeses. Sweet Chenin Blanc makes a sublime dessert wine.

Future bets

We hope it will become more widely recognized – especially if the South African Chenins continue to get better and more complex. The medium-dry whites are currently unfashionable, however; bone-dry and super-sweet will be more widely loved for the foreseeable future.

Pinot Grigio/Pinot Gris

A grape with many faces, Italian Pinot Grigio is popular and even fashionable as an easy-drinking, light white. But try the same grape as Pinot Gris from Alsace or parts of the New World to discover the richer, deeper core of flavour which the Italians are missing out on.

Character

As a very light, insubstantial Italian white – not much! A decent Pinot Grigio (made from high-yielding vines) has a fresh, lemony appeal, with a tangy, sometimes even slightly spritzy hint. Italy produces a huge amount of weaker, simpler Pinot Grigio that sells by the bucket-load in the UK, often at fairly low prices. But Tokay-Pinot Gris from Alsace (same grape) and Pinot Gris from other regions can achieve much more: a rich, smoky, apple-and-peach flavour, with a weighty, full texture and a long finish. Low-cropping vines make the best. It is not generally oaked, but it can (especially from Alsace) have a spicy character, as though subtle additions of smoke, rose-water, and nutmeg were lurking somewhere in there. It can be dry, medium, or sweet. It is at its best from Alsace, in eastern France, where it generally makes rich, opulent, sumptuous, full-bodied whites. Some New World producers are making impressive lookalikes – particularly in New Zealand and Oregon.

When to drink it

Sip well-chilled Pinot Grigio as an easygoing, refreshing, hot-weather wine on its own or with leafy salads or very simple pasta dishes. Richer New World Pinot Gris goes well with white fish, and Alsace's full-bodied Tokay-Pinot Gris is amazingly food-friendly. Try the richest dry/off-dry examples with fine, fatty fare such as roast goose, rich smooth pâtés, egg-and-cheese flans, and cold pork; and bring out a sweet wine with pudding or creamy cheeses.

Future bets

Although Pinot Grigio has been more popular of late, there should be a move toward more serious Pinot Gris eventually as more becomes available (and as Pinot Grigio drinkers get bored).

Sauvignon Blanc

The dry white of choice for many who want a mouth-watering, crisp apéritif. Choose from the lemony, minerally, bone-dry French Sauvignons, then there's the pungent, riper New World style, or the blended sweet wine of Bordeaux. This is one of the most irresistible white wines of all.

Character

Almost as popular as Chardonnay, Sauvignon Blanc seems to be everyone's favourite dry, unoaked white at the moment. But yet again, its character depends on where and how it is made. The most revered Sauvignons used to be those from France's cool Loire Valley: Sancerre and Pouilly-Fumé, Quincy, Reuilly, and Menetou-Salon are make high-class, lean, elegant, lemony dry Sauvignons. These have kept their reputation, but New Zealand's Sauvignons have crashed the party and are now more famous. These are riper, more richly perfumed, and full in flavour, with aromatic gooseberry fruit and not-so-subtle hints of citrus fruit, tomatoes, herbs, and asparagus. Don't miss the great blends, both sweet and dry, with Sémillon in Bordeaux or the exciting newer Sauvignons from other countries, notably South Africa and Chile. Australia makes a little Sauvignon, sometimes blending with Semillon in the western Australian region of Margaret River.

When to drink it

Loire Sauvignon is unbeatable with simple, super-fresh seafood, and goes well with mild cheeses, especially goat's cheese and fresh tomato dishes. New Zealand's wines can take on more spicy, aromatic dishes, so try Thai fish dishes, coriander-scented chicken stir-fries, baked/stuffed tomatoes, or seared tuna with Asian spices. Garlic/mild chilli prawns are excellent with New World Sauvignon, and do try a cool glass with green vegetable dishes, including baked fennel and asparagus with hollandaise sauce.

Future bets

Will get stronger and stronger – in the public's affections, that is, not in pungency and flavour. The French, Chilean, and New Zealand styles are both very popular and well respected at the moment, with South Africa's truly excellent, good-value Sauvignon Blancs next up for more appreciation.

Semillon/Sémillon

Semillon is not a totally easy grape to understand – partly because it so often seems to disappear into a blend with Sauvignon Blanc (mainly in France) or Chardonnay (mainly in Australia). It's also hard to pin down in terms of flavours – a real chameleon, both sweet and dry, young and old.

Character

Sémillon is one of Bordeaux's most important grapes, nearly always blended with Sauvignon Blanc to make superb dry whites, sometimes oaky and built to last. Try the top châteaux of the Pessac-Léognan and Graves regions if you want to sample some of the best rich white wines in the world: the balance between fruit, acidity, and oak is superb. Simpler whites are made all around the wider Bordeaux region and southwest France with the same two grapes; expect a leaner, more grassy style meant for drinking when young. In Australia, Semillon is often blended with Chardonnay (see page 88), but more interestingly it is appreciated here as a quality single varietal, too. The Aussies craft gorgeous, rich Semillons, full of toast, marmalade, honey, and lime flavours. Only they don't taste like that when young. Sometimes oaked, sometimes not, they need years to open up and mellow out. A few good Semillons are made in other corners of the New World, such as South Africa and New Zealand.

When to drink it

Younger, grassier Semillons and Semillon/Sauvignon blends are tasty with leafy salads, grilled white fish, or on their own. Choose oakier, more serious white Bordeaux with fancier, creamier fish or seafood (lobster, scallops, king prawns), and try pairing a mature Australian Semillon with fresh salmon or full-flavoured seafood like crab.

Future bets

Will probably continue to be a relatively dark horse, but it makes a great change from Chardonnay and Sauvignon Blanc. It may become better known if more people switch their allegiance from single varietals to blends in the future.

Riesling

After a period in the doldrums, when Riesling was unfairly associated with cheaper, nastier European wines, it seems to be back in favour again. This is, after all, the wine that "buffs" have always loved, and which makes some of the most refined, longest-lived whites of all.

Character

Making a welcome change from the heavily oaked, powerful styles of white that have dominated for so long, Riesling is naturally lower in alcohol than some white wines and has a more subtle character. It tends to smell orchard-fresh, with crunchy green apples and citrus fruit, perhaps with a hint of blossom, on cool-climate European examples, and a riper, juicy, limey note on New World wines, especially Australian ones. Riesling can be very dry, but is often off-dry, although medium and sweet styles also made. It even makes sparkling wines in some countries (Germany, Austria). The top wines age well, owing to their high acidity, and they acquire an almost petrolly, kerosene hint as they mature. Others simply grow more honeyed and mellow with age. Germany is the variety's first home, and the most elegant, complex, and fascinating German Rieslings reflect terroir more clearly than perhaps any other wines, so the site is crucially important in top bottles. Alsace makes a richer style, while Australia's version is much riper and juicier, but generally high-quality, too. Rieslings from Canada, New Zealand, and Austria are also well worth trying.

When to drink it

The most subtle, delicate Rieslings, generally from Germany's Mosel region, make perfect light apéritifs, especially as their alcohol levels are naturally low (around seven to nine per cent). Otherwise, view this as a grape for white fish, shellfish, and light salads; pair the richer Aussie styles with fish/seafood cooked in richer sauces and spices, though. Medium-dry Rieslings work well with mild cheeses; very sweet ones are brilliant with fruit puddings.

Future bets

Can only continue to enjoy a revival, especially now that many wine drinkers are discovering the wide range of styles available from Europe and the New World. Riesling's naturally low alcohol levels, lack of oaky character, and refreshing, crisp fruit make a nice change from heavier, richer whites.

Viognier

If you like your whites hugely fruity and bursting with peachy aromas and flavours, then Viognier could be the grape for you. Buy carefully, however, as a good Viognier has a rich, opulent perfume of apricots, peaches, and honeysuckle, but a weak one can be disappointingly dull and bland.

Character

Viognier is seriously fashionable right now, probably because it has the generous, fruity character of Chardonnay, but little of the cloying, spicy wood character of over-oaked whites. The fruit character holds sway here – or rather it should, in a concentrated, well-made Viognier. The best come from the Rhône Valley, especially the Condrieu appellation, although be aware that prices tend to be very high for these wines. Less pricey, a decent Côtes du Rhône Blanc should contain a good proportion of Viognier; a peachy perfume is the sign of this. The best examples of whites made from this grape can be stunning. They have been made from the intensely flavoured and perfumed fruit of low-yielding, mature vines, picked at exactly the right time when the grapes are ripe but still have fresh acidity. Making Viognier does require close attention, and although some producers in the South of France and the New World get it right, there are too many dilute versions around. These smell of nothing much, and have a thin flavour vaguely reminiscent of pear-drops.

When to drink it

The best wines are a fine match for creamy chicken and fish dishes, or fruity chicken or vegetable curries. Try one with a mild korma, for example.

Future bets

Should remain "in vogue" for some time. There are plenty of winemakers around the world willing to give this challenging variety a go, so more should appear on the scene from California, Australia, Argentina, and South Africa in time – especially given the current trend for emulating all Rhône styles.

Gewurztraminer & Muscat

Gewurztraminer is a real discovery for many wine-lovers. There's nothing quite like it for an exotic perfume and spicy, unusual flavours. Muscat is another gem, responsible for many sweet wines, both still and sparkling, and for a few interesting dry whites.

Character

A premium Gewurz carries a heady scent of rose-water, peaches, apricots, lychees, melons, ground ginger, Turkish Delight... The flavour should be crisp and fruity with spicy hints. The colour is often a deep gold, and many examples are off-dry, although very dry and very sweet wines are also made. Expect the top wines to come from Alsace in eastern France, where Gewurztraminer is often made in a rich, opulent, and weighty style, with some runners-up from New Zealand, Germany, and Chile. These wines tend to be a little more lean, zesty, and minerally in character.

Muscat, on the other hand, conjures up a simple flavour of green grapes – as mentioned elsewhere in this book, it is perhaps the only well-known wine variety that actually tastes mainly like grapes. There is a large family of related Muscat vines that yields a wide range of sweet, honeyed, luscious styles, sometimes fortified: for example, French Muscat de Beaumes-de-Venise and Muscat de Rivesaltes, Spanish Moscatel de Valencia, and dry Muscats, mainly from Alsace and Australia. The Italian sweet sparkler Asti (which, again, tastes quite grapey) is made from Muscat.

When to drink them

Dry or off-dry Gewurztraminer is a wow with perfumed, exotic dishes such as Thai fish or seafood with lemongrass and coriander, or mussels in coconut milk. The sweet Gewurzes are an exciting match for mild cheeses, or try them with pud. Sweet Muscats make perhaps the most versatile, good-value dessert wines of all; try the French or Spanish ones with fruit puddings in particular. Dry Muscat, served well chilled, is a refreshing apéritif.

Future bets

Both of these grapes tend to be discovered by wine-drinkers looking for something a bit different. As such, they should thrive as the world gets a little bored with the ubiquitous Chardonnay and Sauvignon Blanc.

Other whites

It's well worth casting your net widely to catch other flavours – you can easily get bored by drinking the same old grape varieties. Here are some of the more minor, but nonetheless interesting, white grapes.

Albariño
The specialty of the Rías Baixas region of northwest Spain and a grape that creates some of the country's best white wines. Expect a lime and apricot character, unoaked, with plenty of fresh, crisp acidity. It also pops up as Alvarinho in Portugal, as one of the grapes used for Vinho Verde.

Aligoté
Burgundy's "other" white grape, used occasionally to drum up a light, fresh, apéritif-style wine which, mixed with local *crème de cassis*, is often used as the base for kir.

Colombard
Generally makes slightly bland, dull white wine and is used widely for brandy production, but Colombard can produce fresh, lemony, zesty dry whites that cost relatively little, especially in southwest France and South Africa.

Garganega
An Italian variety that is used in blends for the best Soave, and which, on its own, can produce appealing light whites with notes of apple, lime, and almonds, mainly in northeast Italy.

Grüner Veltliner
Austrian grape, well worth trying for its snappy, dry, mineral style with lemon, grapefruit, and white-pepper notes. The top wines taste richer yet remain succulent and crisp, and age well.

Malvasia
In Italy and Spain, this grape adds a nutty character to blended whites, while on the island of Madeira it is known as Malmsey and makes the best sweet fortified wines produced there.

Marsanne & Roussanne
Two white grapes of the Rhône Valley which are often blended to make slightly floral, nutty wines with a hint of peach. Marsanne is starting to be more widely grown.

Melon de Bourgogne
The grape behind Muscadet, the popular Loire Valley white, the quality of which has improved of late. The best Muscadets are aged *sur lie* – on the lees (yeast sediment) – to add creamy, biscuity hints to a dry, light white.

Palomino

The mainstay of Spain's sherry industry, Palomino makes a fairly basic, uninteresting white wine. The sherry process of yeast and barrel-ageing plus fortification (*see* pages 21 and 129) works wonders, however.

Pinot Blanc

Alsace is the main source of likeable, appley, food-friendly Pinot Blanc. The best wines have a richer, creamy note. As Pinot Bianco and Weissburgunder, it crops up in Italy and Germany, too.

Torrontés

Argentina makes distinctively aromatic, refreshing, zesty whites from this grape. Drink them up while young as apéritif wines, or perhaps with very fresh, light seafood dishes.

Verdelho

Madeira's Verdelho makes medium-sweet fortified wines of high quality. In Australia, it pops up as a dry table white with a juicy, limey character. Worth sampling.

Viura

It's not exactly bursting with character, but the Spanish Viura grape (aka Macabeo) is responsible for lighter, juicier, more modern whites in the Rioja area than the traditional style of white, and it's used in the blend for cava. Also found in southwest France.

Cabernet Sauvignon

It has been described as the king of red grapes – the one that most consistently creates good-quality wine in many parts of the globe. Add to that the fact that Cabernet Sauvignon makes a great partner with Merlot, Shiraz, and other red grapes, and you've certainly got a star.

Character

From some parts of the world, Cabernet Sauvignon just oozes rich, blackcurrant fruit. The Chileans and Argentinians, Bulgarians, Australians, South Africans, and Californians can produce Cabernets that have a rich core of cassis fruit, perhaps with a little plum and blackberry in the mix, but mainly blackcurrant. Sometimes the style is fairly easy-drinking and jammy, but in the main Cabernet makes more powerful, full-bodied wines than this: ones which are rich and robust, often with plenty of spicy oak. The more complex wines from Bordeaux and the New World might have nuances of chocolate, mint, cedar, cigar-box... even eucalyptus. Cabernet Sauvignon is a thick-skinned, small-berry grape, so it's possible to extract a great deal of colour, tannin, and flavour from it. Many are built to age well. Cabernet thrives around the world and creates many brilliant wines, but not always on its own. When discovering Cab, you must try the best blends, as this grape works superbly as part of a duo. In Bordeaux, it is often blended with Merlot to add generous, softer, fruity elements; and in Australia a blend with Shiraz shines. In Italy, it is blended with Sangiovese; in Spain, with Tempranillo. For many fans, the ultimate Cabernet blends are still those of the Médoc in Bordeaux, where elegance and fine balance win out over sheer power and guts. Others will embrace the "blockbuster", mega-rich styles of the top Californian estates. A few cheap and cheerful versions come from Bulgaria.

When to drink it

Cheaper, jammy Cabernets and Cab blends need drinking up soon after purchase. They make versatile partners for a wide range of rich, savoury dishes. The top Cabernets and blends may need plenty of time in the bottle to soften and mellow out, and should be matched with roast lamb or game, or with a fine cheeseboard.

Future bets

Cab can't lose. It is widely grown and deeply popular. Standards are high around the world. It is often seen in a blend, so people are less likely to tire of it than they are of the endless 100 per cent Chardonnays. Just watch out for any underripe, green-pepper versions.

Grenache/Garnacha

Whether you encounter it as Grenache or Garnacha, this grape makes some loveable, juicy, robust red wines, with plenty of bold, ripe flavours and high alcohol levels. Yet it was once used only for cheap plonk.

Character

In southern France, Spain, California, and Australia, Grenache was once the source of "jug" and fortified wines: inexpensive and rough in quality. It was viewed as a variety for blends, with little potential for serious, single-varietal reds. Now that's changing, as winemakers realize that low-cropped, intensely flavoured fruit from this vine can produce a wine that has sweetly ripe plum and blackberry flavours, sometimes with spicy notes. The top wines now come from Priorato and Tarragona in Spain – where as Garnacha this variety makes huge, glowering, concentrated red monsters with high alcohol levels and years to last – and Australia, where Grenache and blends of Grenache with Mourvedre and Shiraz are impressively deep-fruited and satisfying. In the Rhône and southern France, Grenache is still commonly used in red blends, often with Syrah, and it is one of the main players in the blend for Châteauneuf-du-Pape, as well as producing sweet red wines (yes, really) in Banyuls and Maury. Grenache/Garnacha still makes plenty of appealing rosé in Spain and beyond.

When to drink it

The warming, richly fruity flavours of Grenache are enticing, but even at its best this is probably not the most complex of wines. Drink it, then, with hearty, peppery food: red meat stews, sausages, salami, roast game birds. The blends, especially Châteauneuf-du-Pape from the Rhône, can be more serious and would deserve your best red meat roast or finest cheeses. Chilled Spanish *rosado* made from Grenache is delicious with local *jamón* or other tapas dishes; sweet red wine made from it is amazingly good with chocolate puddings!

Future bets

As we've said before, the Rhône is fashionable and Rhône varieties are being planted more widely, so expect Grenache to appear more and more often, especially from Australia and now from California, which is showing interest in this grape, as a single varietal and in blends.

Merlot

Merlot used to be fairly well respected but perceived as Cabernet Sauvignon's poor relation, mainly because it was considered to have the minor role in the classic Bordeaux blend. But its cachet has risen hugely, and now it is one of the most sought-after varieties in the world, made to a high standard in many countries.

Character

Merlot generally yields medium-bodied, merrily fruity red wines with lots of ripe, fleshy, plum flavour. It's easy to enjoy when young but can be made in a richer, oakier, more powerful way in certain parts by talented winemakers. And that's why it is so popular: young, fairly inexpensive Merlot is immediately enjoyable and juicy stuff, but the top examples (from Bordeaux, California, New Zealand, and Chile) are serious wines indeed, so drinkers can follow their favourite grape upmarket, growing more ambitious all the time. As a blending partner for Cabernet, Merlot pads out the rather austere, tannic character of Cab with a more soft and fruity element, and this happy combination makes up much red Bordeaux. In the St-Emilion and Pomerol areas of Bordeaux, however, the claret blend relies much more heavily on Merlot than any other grapes, and the top wines arguably show this grape at its most serious and complex. California is behind some other very impressive takes on Merlot; some are deeply ripe and concentrated, with rich plum and red-berry fruit flavour, although beware: the cheapest West Coast Merlots are rather sweet and bland. Chile perhaps makes the most appealing affordable Merlot. New Zealand's best regions for this grape are the relatively warm Hawke's Bay and Waiheke Island, while South Africa can produce wonderfully intense Merlots and Merlot blends. Cheaper, simpler versions are made in eastern Europe, and lighter, grassier styles in cool northern Italy.

When to drink it

Go for a Merlot or "Bordeaux blend" (Merlot/Cabernet Sauvignon) when eating a wide range of red-meat dishes – especially beef or steak, which seem to go particularly well with this grape. Juicy, ripe but smooth Merlots match red-meat pasta dishes nicely, while richer, more smoky/oaky wines are great with steak-and-kidney pie, roast venison, or fine cheeses.

Future bets

Has probably peaked in terms of sheer icon status, and to some extent been replaced by Pinot Noir and the Rhône reds, but decent Merlot will continue to thrill. It is a classic variety, both in blends with Cabernet Sauvignon and on its own.

Pinot Noir

Winemakers have yearned to make the perfect Pinot Noir for centuries, connoisseurs have long worshipped its finest bottles, and now the wider public seems hugely keen on the soft, silky wines made from this grape.

Character

There are great Pinots and awful Pinots, and the frustrating problem with this grape is exactly how hit-and-miss it is. It's not just a matter of splashing out; you might get a thin, acidic, dull wine even if you invest in an expensive bottle of Burgundy. And it's not even a matter of picking the right region – every one of the cool-climate areas that can make great Pinot Noir also suffers from dud vintages. It can also create the most beguiling, soft, smooth, juicy red wine, which slips down gently, leaving a gorgeous impression of ripe strawberries, cherries, chocolate, and toasted nuts. That's why some people can't get enough of it, despite the many disappointments. And that's why so many winemakers persevere with it, because they love the finest wines it can make, and besides, a brilliant Pinot is clearly the sign of a master craftsman. So this pernickety vine, which hates weather that's too hot, too cold, or too damp, and must be cropped at low yields, keeps being put in the ground in France, California, New Zealand, Chile, South Africa, and Oregon. For most, the best wines are still the top Burgundies, which last for a decade or more, growing more leathery, earthy, forest-fruity, and gamey with age. California can rival this for elegance, while New Zealand makes an impressively fruity, cherry-berry version. Pinot Noir is also one of the three Champagne grapes, and is used for sparkling wines around the world.

When to drink it

Young, simple, fruity Pinot Noir is lovely with fresh salmon (chill the wine slightly before serving to emphasize its freshness) or ham salads. The richer, older wines stand up well to game birds, duck, or creamy cheeses.

Future bets

Going from strength to strength. Hugely admired by serious wine buffs and more generally, perhaps because many are getting a little tired of very powerful, tannic reds and welcome the softer, smoother flavours here. New Zealand is the latest country to go Pinot-mad.

Sangiovese

If you've drunk fine Chianti, then you've enjoyed the Sangiovese grape as part of the blend that goes into this classic Tuscan red. This is arguably Italy's most important variety.

Character

In fact, it rarely appears outside Italy, although the occasional bottle does pop up, for example from California and Argentina, where Italian immigrants brought this vine in the nineteenth century. But otherwise, this is a quintessentially Italian vine, not only the mainstay of Chianti, but also the single variety behind the rich, complex Brunello di Montalcino – and, it must be said, behind a lot of weak, disappointing red destined to be the "house" wine in a downmarket Italian *trattoria*. Yes, Sangiovese can be bland, particularly if cropped at high levels. In a good wine, there should be plenty of ripe strawberry and cherry flavours and a nice twist of sour acidity – just enough to give a refreshing lift to the finish. Most fine Sangiovese and Sangiovese-based wines are medium-bodied, and some have a distinct note of tea-leaf to them – also described as "herby". Pick Chianti Classico for the better-quality wines of this region. Sangiovese is used either alone or in blends (for example, with Merlot) to make big, impressive, oaky, "Super Tuscan" wines as well: the relatively new wave of flagship wines from Tuscany that often break the DOC rules.

When to drink it

As with all decent Italian reds, Sangiovese-based wines are consummately food-friendly. The medium-bodied wines go with a very wide range of savoury food, including pasta with tomato sauces, lasagnes, and other rich, cheesy, baked dishes. Roast game birds such as pheasant are an especially stunning match.

Future bets

Despite the awful standard of most red wine sold in raffia flasks in the 1970s, premium Sangiovese (and indeed Tuscan reds in general) have never quite gone out of fashion, even if they do now come in normal-shaped bottles. At the top end, the finest Chiantis, Brunellos, and Super Tuscans are highly sought after, both in and outside Italy – and they always will be.

Syrah/Shiraz

Yes, it's one and the same grape variety. Known as Syrah in France and Shiraz in Australia, this vine is responsible for some very powerful, spicy winter warmers. Thank goodness it is taken more seriously than it used to be...

Character

... because Down Under, Shiraz was long treated as a "workhorse" grape, fit only for churning out rough or fortified red wines. Then, during the second half of the twentieth century, the Aussies realized what potential it had. Indeed, treated with more care, Shiraz could produce rich, satisfying, serious reds with a powerful, appealing blackcurrant and bramble core, and fascinating notes of black pepper, spice, toffee, chocolate, and cream. The very old vineyards in some Australian regions produce low yields of richly concentrated Shiraz grapes; these generally make the best, most dense and chunky wines of all. Inexpensive blends with Cabernet commonly create a cheerful, easygoing Aussie red. As Syrah in France, the variety was always revered that bit more, but nevertheless it was used for relatively cheap blends in the far south. But in the Rhône Valley, Syrah is highly respected as the grape behind the glowering, monster reds of the northern part of the region. Expect big, robust wines from Côte-Rôtie, Crozes-Hermitage, and St-Joseph, among others, to arrive loaded with ripe black fruit and that distinctive twist of black pepper. Syrah is crucial to the cocktail of grapes that makes up the blend in the southern Rhône, too. Châteauneuf-du-Pape is the most famous appellation here, made mainly from Grenache but with Syrah, Mourvèdre, and others in the mix. Elsewhere, a band of enterprising winemakers in California (dubbed the "Rhone Rangers") are trying out this grape with some success, and it's well worth sampling the new bottles coming from South Africa, New Zealand, and South America, which show great promise.

When to drink it

Apart from the softest French blends, Syrah/Shiraz should be reserved to drink with food – and pretty hearty, peppery, winter-warming food at that. Try it with roast red meats, peppered steaks, rich casseroles, and strong cheeses. A smooth, juicy Aussie Cab/Shiraz is a good idea with a medium-heat meat curry.

Future bets

Its fortunes are set to rise and rise. Already far more popular and well respected than it was a generation ago, Shiraz/Syrah has been taken up by winemakers in many countries recently (*see* above) and the results are looking good. Expect to see many more exciting bottles appear.

Tempranillo

Red Rioja remains Spain's most famous wine, and Tempranillo is the main variety behind those gloriously mellow, red-berry flavours. But this variety appears in many different guises throughout the country.

Character

Love Spanish wine; love Tempranillo. In the Rioja region, to the northwest of the country, this variety has held sway for more than a century. Look out for a soft, juicy, strawberry character, underpinned by creamy vanilla from long ageing in American oak casks. Oak maturation is crucial to traditional Rioja, which can be released, according to the time spent in cask and bottle, as a *crianza*, a more mature *reserva,* or a venerable old *gran reserva*. Nowadays a more modern, fruity style is also made, sometimes labelled *joven* (young), either completely unoaked (*sin crianza*) or with a very short time in cask (*semi-crianza*). Although Tempranillo is the most important and typical grape of Rioja, it is sometimes blended with Garnacha and smaller amounts of Graciano and Mazuelo, or even Cabernet Sauvignon. Outside Rioja, the variety is still hugely important in Spain, but watch out for its pseudonyms. For example, in Ribera del Duero Tempranillo is known as Tinto Fino, and here it makes chunky, long-lived, serious reds with a chocolaty note, while in Valdepeñas and La Mancha it is called Cencibel and makes a range of wines, from the everyday and simple to ripe yet full-flavoured, slightly leathery releases. As Tinta Roriz it is one of Portugal's port grapes, and as Aragonez it produces Portuguese table reds farther south. The Argentinians are starting to come up with a few decent wines from this grape, so watch that space as farther progress is made.

When to drink it

Aged red Rioja is released ready to drink and is softer, more mellow than some imagine. Pair it with sweet, succulent roast lamb for a heavenly marriage of flavours. It also goes well with smooth, rich pâtés and rich cheeses. The big wines of Ribera are delicious with steak, while the lighter, simpler Tempranillos and blends make decent, all-purpose party reds.

Future bets

It will be interesting to see how Argentina (and eventually other countries) fares with this variety in the future, but for now it remains a Spanish classic, and somewhat above the vagaries of fashion. Rioja is riding high at the moment, producing very good quality wines.

Malbec & Nebbiolo

Two slightly less important grapes – not because they cannot produce some excellent wines, but because their success has been somewhat limited to particular wine regions. Nonetheless, give these two a go.

Character

Malbec is a French grape variety, originally a minor variety from Bordeaux used in small quantities in some claret blends, and more widely around the town of Cahors in the south for inky-black, intense, tannic red wines that last for years. But it took the Argentinians to turn it into a star, and now more and more people are discovering Malbec. Grown in Argentina, it makes deeply fruity, bright, ruby-red wines with a noteworthy flavour of black cherry. Although some light, juicy reds are produced, as are some big, oaky/smoky styles, in the main, Malbec is full-bodied but soft and approachable, majoring in ripe fruit and a velvety texture. Many of the best hail from the Mendoza region of the country.

Nebbiolo, meanwhile, is highly regarded for the superb wines it produces in Piedmont, northern Italy. Barolo and Barbaresco are 100 per cent Nebbiolo, and although a bit too chewily tannic when young, they evolve beautifully, eventually opening up to reveal unusual and seductive hints of cherries, dates, chocolate, and even a floral note of roses. Prices are high for the best wines, but that doesn't put off the fervent fans. It is seen very little outside Piedmont.

When to drink them

Premium Argentinian Malbec is a star match with plain, rare steak. It also makes a good wine for pasta with a beef and tomato sauce. A soft, juicy version is also surprisingly delicious with chocolate cake. Mature Nebbiolo makes a lovely partner for roast beef, or try it with an aromatic, truffly dish, or mature, pungent cheeses.

Future bets

Malbec has seemingly sprung up from nowhere to become Argentina's top wine, and as such its future looks assured. It should become better known as Argentina continues to make more impact on the shop shelves. Nebbiolo is set to remain an Italian classic, much revered by fine-wine drinkers both in Italy and abroad who can afford its luxury goods price tag.

Other reds

Here are some more grapes worthy of your attention. They don't all make brilliant wine all the time, and some are very tied to one or two regions, but they each deserve a try.

Barbera
Purveyor of fruity, tangy Italian reds, mainly in Piedmont but more widely in the north of the country. Expect flavours of redcurrants, strawberries, and cherries and a distinctive, refreshingly sour hint on the finish. Argentina makes a little, too.

Cabernet Franc
The "third" Bordeaux red grape after Cabernet Sauvignon and Merlot, Cab Franc is used in the blend there but on its own in the Loire Valley farther north. Here it creates some reds of wonderful elegance and subtlety. The flavours and aromas are raspberries, with a green-leaf – almost grassy – freshness.

Carignan
Not a wine that will ever wow the world, but the best Carignans have an honest, wholesome, earthy/spicy note and plenty of red-berry flavour. It's most often found in the vineyards of southern France and regularly blended with other varieties.

Cinsault
Another grape that usually appears as part of the southern French mix of varieties, but Cinsault occasionally puts in an appearance as a fruity, fresh red, and in South Africa (where it's known as Cinsaut) it can turn out the odd tasty bottle.

Dolcetto
Dolcetto means "little sweet one" and this grape does indeed produce sweetly ripe Italian reds – soft, smooth but with plenty of succulent, red-cherry flavour. It is found almost exclusively in Piedmont, northern Italy.

Gamay
The grape behind Beaujolais. Gamay makes soft, light but refreshing, lively strawberry-flavoured wines. Many are made to be enjoyed while they are young and vibrant, but some richer, more serious Beaujolais exist in the form of the *cru* wines such as Morgon, Moulin-à-Vent, Juliénas, and so on. Weak, sour Beaujolais Nouveau is Gamay at its worst – avoid it at all costs.

Mourvèdre

Around the town of Bandol in Provence, Mourvèdre turns out some distinctively powerful, long-lived red wines, but more generally it is used in blends, particularly in Australia where the intensely fruity Grenache/Mourvedre/Shiraz blend is especially fashionable at present. The Aussies call this grape Mataro and it is grown as Monastrell in Spain.

Negroamaro & Nero d'Avola

Two southern Italian grapes well worth a taste for the more unusual herby/spicy flavours they produce. Negroamaro is responsible for the chocolate-laced, black-fruited Salice Salentino made in Italy's "heel". Nero d'Avola turns out ripe, spicy wines from the sun baked vineyards of the south and Sicily.

Pinotage

South Africa's specialty, created by a cross between Pinot Noir and Cinsaut in the early twentieth century. It used to make far too many rough and nasty reds; now it is treated more skilfully and comes up with lighter, juicy reds (which taste of plums and ripe bananas), as well as serious, oaky styles.

Tannat

Uruguay is the surprising source of chewy, powerful, even beefy reds made from this grape variety. It originally hails from Madiran, in southern France, where it makes heavyweight reds with a dense, black-red colour and bags of tannin. Built to last.

Touriga Nacional

Port is made from a blend of grapes, and this is one of the most important. It is now considered a star variety for making Portugal's new set of superb red wines. These tend to be concentrated and full-bodied, yet rounded and rich in red-berry flavour.

Zinfandel

California's Zinfandel is still sadly used to make bland "white" and "blush" rosés, but thankfully its potential for full-on, aromatic, deeply flavoured reds has been realized, too. The top West Coast Zins are truly thrilling, with masses of pippy, fresh raspberry fruit at the core and a hint of smoky oak.

WINE STYLES

It's not as straightforward as you might think to categorize wines by type. Certainly, the various grape varieties don't always fit neatly into boxes labelled "light whites", "rich reds", and so on. For example, one Merlot might be a fairly light, grassy, tangy red, while another is rich, complex, and chunky. That said, it can be very helpful to have an overall feel for the types of wine out there – mostly so you can pick a bottle that best suits an occasion or dish, but also so you can compare and contrast within each group. Here is a general guide to the most important types of wine – grouped by style.

Crisp, fresh whites

Simple, bland, and weedy, or intensely aromatic, refreshing, and flavourful? Light, dry white wines can be either; it's up to you to choose a style that suits the moment. Certain grape varieties provide more flavour and style than others.

Many light whites are made from grape varieties with little flavour – Trebbiano or Müller-Thurgau, for example. These cheapies probably don't state the grape on the label (it's not worth showing off about). In the hands of a very talented winemaker, you might find a little more character coaxed out of these varieties, but generally it's better to plump for a white made from a more characterful grape, and one that declares that grape proudly on its label. So pick a Riesling, a Sauvignon Blanc, or a better-quality Italian white such as Verdicchio or Lugana. Trade up and away from the boring cheap whites!

Climate is important in this style group. Cooler climates lead to more acidity (freshness, crispness) in grapes and therefore the finished wine, so the best light whites tend to come from cooler spots such as Germany, northern Italy, or France's Loire Valley. A dry, light white should be a mouth-watering, palate-cleansing experience, so pick wines that have this quality. For that reason, too, choose youthful, sprightly, light whites – never old ones. Apart from Riesling, which can age well, light whites need drinking up soon after they are made, so don't hang onto them for long. Serve them well chilled with salads, fresh seafood, simple white fish dishes, or on their own as tangy apéritifs.

Wines to try

European Riesling

Don't underestimate the fine qualities of premium Old World Riesling. With its delicate aroma of apple blossom, its crunchy orchard fruit, and its naturally low alcohol levels, this is a wonderfully elegant, moreish wine. Try German Riesling, of course, and Austrian if you can, as well as the slightly richer examples from Alsace, in eastern France.

Lighter Sauvignon Blancs

French Sauvignon can be beautifully tongue-tingling, dry, and lemony with an almost mineral purity. Be sure to sample the delectable examples from the Loire Valley: Sancerre, Pouilly-Fumé, Quincy, Reuilly, and Menetou-Salon. Sauvignon de Touraine is a cheaper but nonetheless fair-quality Loire dry white. The southwest of France makes lots of easy-drinking, rather grassy Sauvignon Blanc (sometimes blended with Sémillon) as well as more serious white wine (see Semillon on page 115). Austria is the other, rarer source of great Sauvignon Blanc; expect steely, crisp, citric-zesty wines.

Italian whites

There's an ocean of dry Italian white out there, and quality ranges considerably. Sadly, much light Italian white is just plain dull and dilute. Here it really is worth avoiding the cheapest, mass-produced bottles, and trading up to more serious, flavour-packed, expensive wines from reputable producers. Soave, Pinot Grigio, Frascati, and Orvieto all taste much better when made from good-quality, low-yielding grapes by a talented winemaker. Do try Verdicchio, Vernaccia, Arneis, and Lugana, too, for a taste of other light, potentially more interesting Italian whites.

Muscadet

There's still some poor Muscadet about, but standards have been raised recently in the area of northwest France around the city of Nantes, and a higher proportion of bottles now deliver that lemon-and-lime "zing" and hint of creamy yeastiness one expects from Muscadet. Pick a label that says *sur lie* so you know it has been aged on the yeast lees properly. Oh, and crack it open with seafood.

Others

- Vin de Pays des Côtes de Gascogne is a simple, cheap but usually snappily crisp, grassy French country white from the southwest. Made from a blend of Ugni Blanc and Colombard, it must be enjoyed young, fresh, and chilled.
- Sample some dry, peppery Picpoul de Pinet from southern France, if you happen to get the chance.
- Dry Muscat actually tastes like green grapes and can be a brilliant apéritif or match for green vegetable dishes (try asparagus). It is made in Alsace (eastern France), in Italy, Austria, Germany, and, occasionally, in the New World.
- Grüner Veltliner is a worthwhile Austrian specialty with the flavours of juicy grapefruit and white pepper.
- Aligoté is the "other" white grape of Burgundy (after Chardonnay, of course) and the lighter, sprightly base for a million kirs, mixed with a splash of *crème de cassis*.
- Some light, dry English white wines are also well worth a go – try the Bacchus or Madeleine Angevine grapes, for example.

Wines to avoid

Vinho Verde, as the quality is alarmingly patchy; Müller-Thurgau, the grape behind many of Germany's blandest wines (and some of New Zealand's); cheap, dull Italian whites mainly based on Trebbiano; Laski Rizling or Welschriesling (generally substandard central/eastern European whites).

Juicy & aromatic whites

Expect richer flavours and more exotic aromas from these whites. This is where you'll find wines that have the character of a fresh, ripe fruit salad without the rich, oaky character of the full-bodied whites. Some of the most unusual flavours in white wines may be found here...

...alongside some unusual aromas. These wines have enticing, exotic perfumes. Not only are there all those fruit-salad hints – apples, peaches, lychees, melons, gooseberries, and tangerines – but also some other interesting nuances of rose petals, ground ginger, confectionery, and spiced cake. Sometimes it can be frustratingly tricky to know exactly how dry these wines will be. Some have a bone-dry finish, while others are slightly honeyed and off-dry. It's essential that these whites have enough freshness to them. That aromatic white with the enticing bouquet can sometimes taste disappointingly flat and flabby, as though it's missing crisp acidity. The best examples have all the fruit and aroma you could want, *and* a fresh, mouth-watering finish.

These are great whites for matching with food. Whereas the lightest whites have trouble standing up to fuller flavours, and the biggest, richest ones need careful pairing with hearty fare, these medium whites seem to go effortlessly with a vast range of light(ish) savoury dishes, especially those with a hint of sweetness or very pronounced aromas, as in some oriental or Thai cuisine. Always serve these wines chilled.

Wines to try

Gewurztraminer

Alsace Gewurz has all the spicy, rich perfume (lychees, peaches, melon, roses) and weighty ripe fruit you could want. Pick a top producer to avoid the bland, over-scented cheapies, but do try this extraordinary wine. Compare it with Gewurz from other parts of the world, perhaps Germany, New Zealand, or Chile. Match it with exotic dishes, especially Thai cuisine.

New World Sauvignon Blanc

A highly aromatic, zesty mouthful of gooseberry and lime, asparagus and tomato leaf; it's hardly a light white! Kiwi Sauvignon is like the French style with the volume turned up. Try South African Sauvignon if you fancy something in between.

Chenin Blanc

Highly fruity variety with flavours of apple and quince or, from South Africa, more like limes and guava. From the Loire Valley, Chenins dry, medium, and sweet can be majestic and evolve wonderfully over time into honeyed, toasty depths. Try a top example from

Vouvray or Savennières to see what we mean. Cape Chenins tend to be more frivolous but they are succulent, crowd-pleasing party whites.

Unoaked or lightly oaked Chardonnay

Unlike the big, rich, oaky Chardonnays, those with no oak, or perhaps with a small proportion aged briefly in oak, focus on fresh fruit flavours. Zesty citrus fruit and a hint of pineapple and peach make for a succulent, medium-bodied white that's useful to match with creamy pasta or eggy quiches.

New World Riesling

A much more limey, ripe, sunny blast of flavour than you get from European Riesling (less subtle, more alcoholic, too). Australian and New Zealand examples are especially good, and the top ones age well.

Albariño

Spain's best white wine, made in the Rías Baixas region of Galicia, in the northwest, close to the Atlantic coast. The Albariño grape produces whites that have fresh, tangy peach and lime flavours and no oak. Try them with white fish dishes or squid.

Pinot Blanc

Consummately food-friendly, medium-bodied white wines with a soft, appley, slightly creamy quality. Alsace has the best Pinot Blanc; there it is brought out to match quiches and savoury flans.

Tokay-Pinot Gris

Alsace's take on Pinot Grigio produces a much more serious wine with arresting aromas of spiced baked peaches and honey – but no oak. Sometimes medium or sweet, and sometimes lacking in acidity, nonetheless the greatest TPGs are amazingly weighty and rich without any use of oak, and terrific with pâtés, creamy fish, and chicken dishes.

Irsai Oliver

A cheap eastern European version of Gewurztraminer, if you like, with a similarly exotic rose-petal and lychees aroma but a less complex flavour. A good introduction to spicy whites, though, as long as you buy a fresh young wine and drink it up quickly.

Wines to avoid

Californian Fumé Blanc (oaked Sauvignon Blanc), unless you know you like this style of Sauvignon. Although more vibrant, snappy examples are being made today, some are still oddly smoky, savoury, and sweetish in style; cheap Gewurztraminer, which can smell a bit like nasty perfume, with little flavour or acidity; basic Anjou Blanc from the Loire Valley – Chenin Blanc at its worst.

Full-bodied whites

Enjoy the richest, ripest, creamiest white wines at the right moment – that's not as an apéritif or with a leafy salad, but with luxurious seafood, roast turkey, or wild salmon in a creamy sauce. It's all about context, and in the right one, these wines are just the ticket.

Some wine-lovers swear by rich, oaky Chardonnay or mature, toasty Semillon or ripe, peachy Viognier; others swear they can't stand them. The biggest white wine styles provoke strong opinions, but it doesn't have to be like that. Just serve them at the right time. These are certainly not light lunch wines for an easygoing meal alfresco, but crack open a full-bodied white with classic roast chicken or a creamy prawn curry on a cold winter's evening and suddenly you'll see the point. They are not meant to provide instant apéritif refreshment; they are meant to go with rich, hearty food – almost as a red should.

These whites should have plenty of generously ripe fruit flavours – probably hot-climate, tropical fruits like peaches, pineapples, mangoes, and oranges. Look out, too, for those hints of oak (vanilla, cream, butter, even a touch of sawdust) and some spicy notes of clove or nutmeg. Toasted/roasted nuts appear in some of these wines, but this oak/toasty quality should only enhance the wine – not overwhelm it. Beware big whites with too much oaky flavour, as they can taste overpoweringly woody, usually at the expense of fresh fruit flavours.

Despite their ripe fruit and powerful nuances, look out for good crisp acidity, too, which gives a clean, fresh finish to the wine. Everything should be in good balance; the best big whites are powerful, but not heavy-handed and clumsy. Beware cloying, slightly sugary wines. Ideally, most of the following examples should have a fairly dry finish, despite their huge, sweetly ripe come-on.

Wines to try

Oaked Chardonnay

The Chardonnay grape takes especially well to oak, and a good example that has been fermented and/or aged in fine oak barrels must have all the natural exuberant fruit of this grape, only filled out and given extra body and complexity by oaky hints of nuts, toast, brioche, cream, and vanilla. Yum! The very best (and most subtle, if full-bodied) arguably still hail from Burgundy, in France, where the top winemakers are brilliant at marrying Chardonnay with oak. Pick and choose carefully, however, as cheap white Burgundy can be disappointingly bland. Great (and more everyday) examples are also made in Australia, California, New Zealand, Italy, Spain, Chile, and South Africa. Check out good-value, ripe Chardonnays from the South of France, Argentina, and eastern Europe. Drink with roast chicken or turkey, smoked salmon, or any fish served with a rich, buttery sauce.

Semillon & Semillon blends

Australia makes impressive Semillon that tastes rather lean and grassy when young but acquires amazing honeycomb, lime marmalade, and toast character with age. These aged Semillons are usually not oaked and have a dry finish. Less serious, but often tasty and ripe, the Semillon/Chardonnays from Down Under make an easy-drinking, juicy match for creamy curries and other rich, savoury food. Sem/Chard blends are one big white that does slip down easily at parties. Sémillon from Bordeaux, in France, is often blended with Sauvignon Blanc to make some of the best whites around, often carefully oaked, impressively refined, and built to age well.

Viognier

Anyone who likes Chardonnay's bright, fruity character but gets tired of choosing it all the time should give Viognier a whirl. Richly perfumed and with a distinctive juicy note of peach and apricot, Viognier is an exciting grape variety in the hands of a talented team, but it can be a let-down if the grapes aren't picked at exactly the right time, or if the winery chooses to make a cheap and bland version. Top examples should send you reeling; the honeysuckle and apricot perfume is second-to-none among white wines, and that peachy flavour should be concentrated, rich, and weighty in texture. The most serious and intense are mainly from Condrieu and Château-Grillet in France's Rhône Valley, but some half-decent ones are made in the South of France, Argentina, Australia, and South Africa.

Roussanne & Marsanne

The duo behind the blended white wines of the Rhône Valley, which taste less of fruit but more of nut kernels, beeswax, nutmeg, and aniseed. Intriguing wines to try with creamy-sauced chicken and fish dishes.

White Rioja

Some modern, lighter whites are being made in Rioja, Spain, these days, but that doesn't mean the heavily oaked, vanilla-tinged traditional Riojas have disappeared completely. Some bodegas (wineries) still swear by this style; aged in American oak casks for years, it takes on a distinctly sawdusty, vanilla character. Try with smoked fish.

> ### Wines to avoid
> Retsina, the Greek wine made with added pine resin, unless you're in "anything goes" holiday mode; cheap and nasty basic Bourgogne Blanc (Burgundy); the most crass and oaky-sweet, cheap New World Chardonnays and Sem/Chard blends.

Soft, tangy reds

They don't seem popular at the moment, but light reds can be delightful and refreshing. Delightful because of their fresh, juicy, and soft fruit flavours and sweet aromas; refreshing because they can be quaffed more freely and easily than heavier reds, and used to wash down a vast range of savoury snacks.

Think of light reds as sitting somewhere in between the fruitiest rosés and the medium-bodied reds. This may sound obvious, but so many people make the mistake of missing out on smooth, fruity, soft reds while quaffing plenty of riper reds and trendy pinks. Once again, it's a case of picking the style of wine that suits the moment. There are some occasions when the more subtle, silky reds are unbeatable. Take parties, for example. It's a common mistake to serve ripe, tannic red at a drinks party. Hefty reds are just not easy to drink in quantity; they soon taste overwhelming, especially without richly flavoured food. Light reds slip down easily, though, and are much less likely to clash with creamy cheeses, pasta salads, pickles, relishes, or cold salmon. They go particularly well with the classic party spread: pizza slices, sausage rolls, medium cheeses, pies, roast chicken legs, etc.

Here's another great moment for a light red. You're eating outside, dining on fresh fish or cold chicken and salad. You can't possibly have a red wine, can you? Yes, actually. A lightly chilled soft red would be spot-on, especially with cold meat or a rich fish like salmon or fresh tuna.

Wines to try

Beaujolais

Tart, dilute Beaujolais Nouveau can be horrid, but don't let that put you off trying good-quality reds from the same region: southern Burgundy. Gamay is the grape behind Beaujolais, and at its best it produces tangy, refreshing, red-berry flavours galore, especially strawberry and red cherry. The soft character is partly to do with carbonic maceration (or "whole grape fermentation"). The key is to trade up from horrid Nouveau and even basic Beaujolais to wines labelled Beaujolais-Villages, made from grapes grown in superior sites, or even better, those from a named village site to the north of the region such as Juliénas, Morgon, or Brouilly.

Light Pinot Noir

This grape variety can make richer, riper reds (see pages 118–19) but should always be soft and velvety-smooth. Lighter, youthful Pinots should also show fresh strawberry flavour: wild strawberries, with a little raspberry and plum. Top wines come from Burgundy, but try the lighter, simpler examples from Alsace. In Germany, as Spätburgunder, Pinot makes decent, quaffable reds. For a slightly richer yet smooth version, try New Zealand's excellent Marlborough Pinots, which are rich without being chunky, and have a distinct cherryish note.

Loire reds

The Loire Valley is more famous for its white wines, but the reds made there from Cabernet Franc are soft, fruity, underrated gems. Expect raspberry and pepper and a certain green-leafiness. The vineyards of Chinon and Bourgueil produce many of the best bottles.

Light Italian reds: Teroldego, Bardolino, Valpolicella, and Dolcetto

Valpolicella, from the Veneto area, is made from a blend of grapes; try a premium, richer Valpol with good cheeses. More pricey but quite delicious. Dolcetto is a grape variety from Piedmont with a soft, tangy, red-cherry flavour – a great match for tomato dishes.

Bonarda

Argentina's soft, light reds are mainly made from the Bonarda grape. It's never going to win any awards for depth and complexity but the best Bonardas have a moreish, fruity quality that makes them contenders for a good party red.

Wines to avoid

The most basic, cheap red Burgundy; underripe reds with a green, stalky character; cut-price Valpolicella; Beaujolais Nouveau and ordinary Beaujolais; almost all English reds; old light reds.

Medium, ripe reds

It's difficult to imagine a wine-lover who doesn't enjoy well-balanced, medium-bodied red wine. What's not to like? Here you should find plenty of ripe fruit, a firm (but not powerful or heavy), chewy structure, and a good balance of oak, acidity, and tannin. As for food-matching, these are versatile reds that make some heavenly marriages with favourite dinner-party dishes.

Many of the classic European reds fall into this category: French Merlot, Rioja, Chianti, and southern Italian reds. New World reds are often too heavy and rich to appear here, but a few juicy, medium-bodied Pinot Noirs, Cabernet/Shiraz blends, and Malbecs fit the bill. The key to a good medium red is a fine balance. These wines should not be awkward, angular, or difficult in any way. They should not have heavy, chewy tannins or lots of big, raw oak. Ideally, they have ripe, rich fruit flavours (blackcurrant, plum, strawberry, raspberry) supported by a fine thread of tannin, well knit into the general fabric of the wine. Acidity should keep the wine fresh but not tart and tangy, although a slight twist of sourness on the finish makes for especially food-friendly medium reds (like Chianti from Italy), as it cuts through any fattiness.

Some medium reds are fairly straightforward, uncomplicated wines, meant for washing down good, honest food, while others are more serious wines that will age well and have multiple layers of flavour and texture. Yet they should all be food-friendly. Whether you order pasta in meat sauce, roast duck, lamb chops, vegetarian lasagne, or a cheese ploughman's, a glass of medium red should go with it. Avoid pairing these wines with fish and seafood (salt cod is the exception) or leafy salads, but otherwise medium reds are a safe bet, especially when more than one dish is on the table.

Wines to try

Merlot

Except for the chunkiest, meatiest Merlots (mainly expensive wines from Bordeaux, Italy, California, and other New World countries), this grape makes wines that can be described as medium-bodied, fruity, ripe, and inviting, with a rich aroma and flavour of plums, red-berry compôte, and perhaps a spicy hint of oak. Do try the Merlot and Merlot blends of Bordeaux and southwest France, but also the vibrant examples from southern France, Spain, and especially Chile, which makes terrific, fresh, slightly chocolatey examples.

Tuscan reds

Chianti Classico from Tuscany, in central Italy, is still going strong. A good example is just about the best kind of medium-bodied red there is, with plenty of ripe cherry and strawberry flavour, some (but not too much) mouth-filling concentration and structure, and a fresh finish. The principal grape used in the blend is Sangiovese. Do try Brunello di Montalcino (pure Sangiovese) and Vino Nobile di Montepulciano (mainly Sangiovese).

Other Italian reds

Italy has a treasure-trove of its own grapes, including Barbera, which makes slightly sour, deeply fruity red in the north. In the southern part of the mainland there's a happy crop of medium-bodied reds. These wines, made from grapes such as Nero d'Avola, Primitivo, and Negroamaro, have blackberry, plum, and raspberry juiciness, with intriguing hints of wild herbs, pepper, and spice. They tend to be rich but relatively smooth.

Rioja

Surprised? Many think of Rioja as full-bodied, but in fact most examples are too mellow for that. Apart from a few modern, unoaked young wines (which don't taste very typical of the region), most reds made in this bit of northern Spain are aged in oak casks and in the bottle before release. The idea is that the wine is sold mature and ready to drink; in the case of *reservas* and *gran reservas*, that means soft and mellow. The main grape is Tempranillo, and the wines usually taste of strawberries and vanilla-ish wood spice.

New World Pinot Noir

Be aware that the richest, plushest Pinot Noirs from California, New Zealand, and Chile are riper and more mouth-filling than the lightest styles, with a lot more plummy clout.

Australian Cabernet/Shiraz blends

We all know Aussie reds are generally big and chunky (see pages 120–1), but some cheap, cheerful Cab/Shiraz blends are juicy, smooth, and easy-drinking: more medium than full. A little too jammy, perhaps, but fine for everyday drinking.

Malbec

Argentina is doing great things with this French grape (hardly famous in France), producing fairly soft but intensely flavoured reds with black cherry and chocolate character. Some Malbecs are more chunky and oaky. Great with steak.

Pinotage

South Africa's very own grape makes reds which range in style and price, but many are medium-bodied, with a red-berry note, and perhaps a hint of banana and/or tomato.

Wines to avoid

Cheap, own-label Pinotage; the most basic *trattoria* Chiantis; Spanish table plonk (*vino de mesa*) trying to emulate Rioja; unripe Merlot from cool-climate spots (these can taste green and stalky); big-brand, "bargain" Californian Merlot: too sweet, too oaky.

Full-bodied reds

Just like the most powerful white wine, the monster reds need bringing out at the right moment. Don't crack one open without thinking hard; is this really the time for a big, flavour-packed red, bristling with dark berry fruit, spices, and tannin?

If you're having rich food, then the answer may well be yes. These are not wines to fuel a food-free drinks party, as they will taste too strong and overwhelming. But paired with roast lamb or rare steak, some hard, sharp cheeses, or a hearty stew, they come into their own. The full-bodied reds have the guts to stand up to serious food, and you'll find that their chewy tannins seem more mellow and soft when matched with rich protein.

So there's nothing like a big red on a cold winter's day – Sunday lunch or the Christmas feast spring to mind. But these are not only cold-weather wines. Barbecuing lamb cutlets or pork chops? Forget light, soft, typically summery reds: this is one moment when you do need to roll out a big gun to match the food – despite the warm, sunny day.

Talking of temperature, never serve a full-bodied red slightly cool, as you might a lighter red. Tannic, firm wines do not taste good when cold. Indeed, if you keep your reds in a cool spot, like a cellar, be sure to bring them to room temperature before enjoying them. You may want to aerate them (help them to "breathe") in order to a) open up the aroma, b) mellow the flavour, and c) remove the sediment if it has collected in the bottle. If so, pour the wine gently into a decanter (for more on decanting, *see* pages 32–3) or simply swoosh it around in a big red wine glass to aerate it instantly.

Wines to try

Big Cabernets

Cabernet Sauvignon has the ability to produce superb, full-bodied reds, either on its own or in blends with other varieties. Top Bordeaux reds, especially those from reputable estates in the Médoc region, are often Cabernet-rich, and have a majestic flavour of blackcurrant, plum, and cedar. Try the best Cabernet Sauvignons from California (if you are prepared to splash out), as these can be extremely concentrated and long-lived, and don't miss Australia's Cabernets, which are generally huge in structure and long in flavour but vary in character interestingly from region to region. South Africa is another source of impressive Cabernet Sauvignons and Cab blends, and for good value, try Chile's ultra-fruity top wines.

Shiraz/Syrah

The whopping great, peppery reds of the northern Rhône are made almost entirely from Syrah. Give Côte-Rôtie, Cornas, and the other parts of the north a whirl if you like your reds black and intense. And Australia's best Shiraz? Packed with cassis, leather, toffee, pepper, and spice – enough said.

Rhône & southern French reds

The southern Rhône uses a cocktail of grape varieties, including Grenache and Syrah, to make ripe, purple reds, the most famous of which is Châteauneuf-du-Pape. In the far south, plenty of big, full-bodied reds are made, especially in Minervois and Corbières.

Portuguese reds

Don't miss the impressive red wines coming out of the Douro Valley in northern Portugal. Yes, this is port country, but a whole crop of unfortified, intensely flavoured reds are also being made, based on the blend of port grapes. Quality is high. Check out the reds of the Dão and Bairrada regions of Portugal for more big red treats.

Zinfandel

It can be made into "blush" or white wine, and even as a basic, inexpensive, jammy red Zinfandel hardly falls into the full-bodied category. But decent, concentrated Californian red Zin is a completely different beast, loaded with pippy raspberry fruit and a twist of pepper. A great one for the barbecue.

Others

- Barolo and Barbaresco from Piedmont in northern Italy should be sampled for the way they manage to be huge and mouth-filling, yet graceful and smooth. Try to spot the famous scent of truffles, tar, and roses.
- Uruguay is making a mark with its chewy, dense reds made from the Tannat grape.
- Grenache, the big-hearted, flavour-packed grape behind southern Rhône blends (see above) is now impressing the critics with its powerfully concentrated, long-lived Spanish wines, especially the extremely strong, sweetly ripe wines from up-and-coming regions such as Priorato and Tarragona.
- Other Spanish reds can be grand and majestic, especially those made in Ribera del Duero, Rioja's neighbour to the southwest. The grapes used are mainly Tempranillo (here called Tinto Fino).

> ### Wines to avoid
> Happily, most big reds are generally reliable in quality, but don't expect them to be cheap. The most mundane, inexpensive ones might be a bit jammy and sweet-tasting, though. You'll have to trade up a bit, particularly in classic "big red" areas such as Bordeaux, California, and the Rhône. Cheap isn't always cheerful, especially in this style group.

Rosé: back in the pink

The richest styles of pink wine are a lot like light reds: deep cerise in colour and full of ripe, lip-smacking, red-berry fruit. The very lightest are almost like a white: ultra-pale and more tangy than juicy. So when should you plump for which style of pink?

The style of your rosé depends largely on where it comes from, and which grapes have been used to make it. If it is from a cool-climate area, such as the Loire Valley or northern Italy, the pink wine is likely to be light, delicate, and refreshing, while a rosé from the south of France, California, or Australia will be made from riper grapes, and look and taste fuller, riper, juicier. A grape variety such as Grolleau (used for rosé in the Loire) carries less flavour and aroma than one like Grenache (used for rosé in Spain, southern France, and Australia), so that makes a difference, too. And how the rosé is made counts for a lot. Rosé is produced mostly by letting the colour from the red grape skins soak with the juice for a controlled period; during this time, the pink colour leaches off into the juice. It's up to the winemaker to decide how long the skin stays in contact with the juice, and this is another factor that dictates what the end result tastes like.

Chill all rosés. Even the ripest should be served with a light chill to bring out the succulent fruity flavours. But the richest are wonderfully food-friendly and can be matched with cold cuts (not just chicken and turkey, but cold ham, pork, and even duck), roasted garlic vegetables, and even used to wash down rich, sweetish, spicy seafood dishes (especially if the rosé is off-dry, which many are), creamy, mild curries, or chicken and prawn stir-fries.

Select a lighter, more elegant pink wine as an apéritif or for drinking on its own (perhaps in the garden on a hot summer's day?). Medium-bodied styles (for example, pink Merlot from Bordeaux or Rioja's *rosado*) are just perfect for matching with light, easy dishes such as leafy salads, fresh seafood, or white fish, starters of cold *jamón* or grilled vegetables. Match your rosé to the moment and you can't go wrong.

Wines to try

Light pinks

The Loire Valley makes some elegant, well-balanced rosés, and the good news is that the overall quality has improved a lot in recent vintages. *See* page 18 for more on which to pick from the Loire. Italy makes some lighter, tangy rosés as well, as does England occasionally. The Californians put out bland, slightly sweet, off-white and blush wines which hardly look pink at all – not the best choice if you want interesting flavours.

Medium pinks

Expect medium-bodied rosés with a delightfully fresh, strawberry-and-cream flavour from Bordeaux. The best Spanish *rosado* comes from Rioja and Navarra, but you should find some tasty bottles from other parts of the country. Enjoy the fresh, summery, red-cherry and raspberry flavours. Chile makes a few rosés that taste similar.

Fuller pinks

In this category, choose from rich, deeply coloured rosé wines from Australia and the new-wave pink producers in California.

Champagne & sparkling wines

From France to New Zealand, winemakers across the world are trying their hand at the intricate art of making wine sparkle. There's Champagne, of course, in northeast France, where arguably some of the very best fizz is made. In New World countries such as Australia they tend to look to Champagne for both their methods and choice of grapes. Here's a guide to the best and most famous sparklers.

France: Champagne

Just over 300 million bottles of Champagne are now produced each year. The word "Champagne" can be used only for wines made in the Champagne region of northeast France, and there are strict rules about the production method there. Three grape varieties can be used: the white grape Chardonnay and the red grapes Pinot Noir and Pinot Meunier. The method of making Champagne is by a second fermentation in the bottle. A light wine is made and then bottled and sealed with a little yeast and sugar to trigger refermentation. The bubbles are created and trapped in the liquid during this second fermentation. Over a long period of months (if not years), the yeast sediment in the bottle imparts a characteristic bready, creamy, biscuity quality to the wine. It is eventually removed by a painstaking, gradual process: a series of gentle twists turns the bottle upside-down; the sediment collecting in the neck is frozen and then popped out like a plug; then the bottle is topped up and sealed. This method is now used to make premium sparkling wines all over the world; the words *méthode traditionnelle* on a label legally denote the practice.

Champagne styles

DRY TO SWEET
- **Extra brut** Bone-dry, having been topped up, post-*disgorgement*, with still wine to which no sugar syrup has been added.
- **Brut** Most of the decent non-vintage (NV) Champagnes are brut, although levels of dryness tend to vary according to the house style.
- **Extra-dry** Edging toward medium-dry.
- **Sec** As this style is best described as medium, its literal translation of "dry" is misleading, to say the least.
- **Demi-sec** Again, confusing nomenclature as the wonderfully subtle sweetness of the best demi-sec Champagnes makes them ideal partners for many light, fruit-based desserts.
- ***Riche/doux*** Rich and fabulously sweet.

BLANC DE BLANCS

This is Champagne that is made solely from white Chardonnay grapes. Usually a finer and more tenacious style, with a certain femininity that sets it apart from the classic blend.

BLANC DE NOIRS

As you'll probably have guessed, these Champagnes are exclusively the territory of the black varieties Pinot Noir and Pinot Meunier. They often have a slight pinky tinge due to their black skins, and are usually rich and full-bodied in style.

NON-VINTAGE (NV)

All Champagne houses produce a non-vintage Champagne that expresses their own house style perfectly, and the idea is that it'll taste exactly the same whenever you buy it. In order to achieve this, the base wines of the current vintage are blended with several "reserve" wines from previous years, before bottling, prior to the second fermentation.

Champagne by any other name

Various Champagne houses, keen to jump on the New World bandwagon, have set up camp in Australia, New Zealand, California, and Argentina. Look out for the house name on the label and you'll get the best of both worlds: tradition and experience as well as sunshine and innovation.

VINTAGE

Sometimes the harvest is so good that it's possible for the *chef de cave* to create a Champagne that perfectly expresses the house style without any need for the addition of reserve wines. In such years a "vintage" Champagne will be made and the label will carry the year of the vintage. These wines are meant to age well for years.

PRESTIGE CUVEE

The one wine that crowns a range and offers the ultimate in terms of luxury, quality, and, indeed, price. Produced using grapes from the best years, from the best vineyards, and with all the care that it's possible to lavish on a single wine. Usually vintage-dated, they are very expensive, unsurprisingly.

Is Champagne always the best choice?

There are good Champagnes and bad, just as there are some wonderful and some utterly dire sparkling wines being made worldwide. The big brand names of Champagne are usually pretty consistent – they have to be, as their livelihoods depend on it. But that consistency comes at a price. Equally, you'll find some great small-grower Champagnes, particularly under supermarket own-labels. If you want value for money, then head for the New World, where traditional-method wines can be as good as, if not better than, many Champagnes – and at usually half the price. The warmer climate means that these wines tend to be fruitier and fuller in style, very appealing to those who don't like anything too sharp, or to those drinking fizz all night.

ROSE CHAMPAGNE

Made in one of two ways: either by blending in a little still red wine from the region before bottling, or by allowing the skins of the black grapes to stay in contact with the juice just long enough for some of the colour to seep into the wine. Soft, red-fruit flavours and a rich, full body make rosé a good match for food.

France: Crémant

Most of the classic regions of France produce their own version of a *crémant*. When, in the late 1980s, the EU stopped the use of the term *méthode champenoise* on the labels of wines made outside the Champagne region, *crémant* was adopted to describe traditional-method sparkling wines produced throughout France. Made in the same way as Champagne, and with quality a top priority, these *crémant* wines are a good bet if you're looking for a decent French alternative to the real thing. The grape varieties and terroirs vary from region to region, but all have strict controls on production. The main regions are Alsace, Die, Bourgogne (Burgundy), Loire, Limoux, Bordeaux, and Jura.

Spain: Cava

When we think of sparkling wine and Spain, the first word that immediately springs to mind is cava – and so it should, considering that it accounts for ninety to ninety-five per cent of Spain's total sparkling-wine production. The word *cava* means "underground cellar" in Spanish, and from 1970 it was adopted as the generic name for sparkling wines made by the traditional method. Cava may be made by the traditional method, but the grapes must come from listed vineyards. The traditional trio used in white cava are local varieties, little known outside Spain, and certainly not names we'd easily recognize: Xarel-lo, Parellada, and Macabeo. Although it is made by the traditional method and is, at best, a refreshing glass of fizz, cava will never hit the heights of good Champagne. Cava is, however, a great-value, reliable party or "everyday" fizz. So when you're planning your next brunch party, don't waste decent Champagne on the all-essential Buck's fizz. Instead, mix equal quantities of cava with freshly squeezed orange juice.

Italy: Prosecco

This is the name of both the grape and the Italian sparkling wine made from it in the cool, hilly region just north of Venice. Prosecco is a fresh, light, and intensely aromatic wine with primary fruit and floral flavours (apricots, apples, and jasmine) and relatively low levels of alcohol. Valdobbiadene and Conegliano are the places where you'll find the best Prosecco being produced, so look out for these names on the label.

Safe popping

When opening any sparkling wine, make sure that the bottle is well chilled. Hold it with the neck pointing away from you at a forty-five-degree angle and, with one hand held firmly over and around the cork to counter the pressure of the bubbles, twist the base of the bottle with the other hand in an anti-clockwise direction, until the cork removes itself with a gentle *phfutt*.

Italy: Asti

This is a simple, sweetish, relatively low-alcohol sparkler that goes well with pudding or with a bowl of strawberries and cream in the garden. After the grapes are pressed in the winery, the must is chilled and fermented only when the wine is required for bottling. In this way the intense fruit character and aroma of the Moscato Bianco (Muscat) grape variety are preserved. Its superior, less mass-produced cousin is the aromatic, delicately fizzy Moscato d'Asti from Piedmont, in northeast Italy.

Germany: Sekt

The Germans manage to knock back almost four litres (7 pints) per capita of fizz each year. A lot of this, however, comes in the form of very low-quality, mass-produced, branded Sekt. The bulk is made from cheap base wine sourced outside Germany and then fermented in large tanks; the result is quite basic, fizzy wine. However, a few higher-quality Sekts are produced in Germany (and Austria, for that matter). These are usually made either from Riesling or one of the Pinot grape varieties, and say Deutscher Sekt on the label, which means the base wine is German. The real stars are vintage Sekts from a particular region or even a specified vineyard.

New World sparklers

There are simply loads of delicious sparkling wines to choose from today, many hailing from newer wine-producing countries. Generally speaking, the top wines are traditional-method ones, made from Chardonnay and Pinot Noir.

New Zealand

The sparklers of New Zealand are especially impressive. The cool, sunny climate of the Marlborough region, on New Zealand's South Island, creates the ideal grapes for sparkling wine, and the typical style is simple, fresh, and fruity with pure, crisp flavours. Good value.

California

Certain Californians have dedicated themselves to high-quality sparkling wine production, and top labels from the state are impressively rich and creamy – possibly the best outside Champagne, though with a price tag to match.

Australia

Australia now has some delicious sparklers, made with fruit from cooler-climate spots of land, although the very cheapest Aussie fizz is not recommended. Do, however, try the Australian sparkling reds – mainly Shiraz – if you get the chance. These have juicy, off-dry, red-berry flavours and are great fun.

South Africa

Some traditional-method sparklers are made in South Africa. These are known as méthode cap classique (MCC) and are generally decent quality.

England

Finally, don't miss England's up-and-coming bubblies. The climate is cool, some of the soils are similar to Champagne, and now the winemakers are getting sparkling styles right. Today, English fizz really can compete with the rest of the world.

Sweet & fortified wines

Don't make the common mistake of underrating sweet and fortified wines. They may not be terribly fashionable, but so what? These styles of wine give us some of the most intense and exciting flavours of all. And just a little of these concentrated elixirs goes a long way. Here's a rundown of the best in the world.

Australia

Liqueur Muscat is an Australian specialty, produced in the Rutherglen region of Victoria. Expect a wine that tastes like liquid raisins, with notes of spice, toffee, and fruit cake. This is warming, hearty stuff, to be served at room temperature on cold nights, perhaps with a sticky, rich pud. Other sweet wines are made in Australia, most commonly botrytized Semillon, an unfortified confection that can be great value for money. Aussie sweet Semillon tastes of peaches and butterscotch – a richer, riper version of Bordeaux's sweet wines, perhaps.

France

Golden, luscious, fortified Muscats with a honeysuckle scent and fresh finish appear from southern France in the form of *vins doux naturels*. The most famous is Muscat de Beaumes-de-Venise, closely followed by Muscats from Rivesaltes and Frontignan. Often great value for money, these make versatile dessert wines, either on their own or with many fruity puddings, or try matching them with smooth pâtés. Try sweet red Banyuls, too (made from Grenache) – especially with chocolate. Some of the most opulent and majestic sweet wines in the world are made in Sauternes and Barsac around Bordeaux, where botrytis rot affects the Sémillon and Sauvignon Blanc grapes. Monbazillac is a cheaper alternative. And in the Loire, beautifully crisp yet sweet wines are created with Chenin Blanc. These have a distinctive, fresh apple and quince quality, and the best age for decades into honeyed, mellow oldies.

Germany

Great dessert wines are produced here from late-harvest and nobly rotten grapes, with fresh, crisp acidity and subtle, complex flavours to balance the onslaught of sweetness. The best are obtained from Riesling. Beerenauslese on a label indicates this sweet style, but even sweeter are Trockenbeerenausleses, while the most rare and concentrated of all are Eisweins, made from the concentrated juice of winter-picked, semi-frozen grapes. Try sweet German wines created with the citrus-fruity Scheurebe grape, too.

Hungary

Tokaji, the "dessert wine of kings", is one of the most wonderful wines in the world. Made mainly from the Furmint grape, it tastes of candied peel, toffee, and marmalade. The wines are graded according to how much botrytized grape paste has been added; see the number of *puttonyos* (literally "buckets") on the label and aim for one with at least three *puttonyos*, preferably more. Good-quality, chilled Tokaji is fabulous with chocolatey, nutty desserts.

Italy

Produces the well-known and highly respected (at least from top producers) *vin santo*, or "holy wine", which is made from dried grapes that yield a concentrated syrup. Flavours are luscious, with barley sugar, citrus-fruit peel, and nuts commonly recorded in tasting notes. Dunk cantuccini biscuits into chilled *vin santo* at the end of dinner for one of the best taste sensations on earth.

Portugal

The land of port, which hails from the upper Douro Valley in the north. Here, red grapes bake on steep vineyard slopes and produce (in great years) the powerful, headily rich vintage port, which takes years to mature, as the robust, deeply flavoured, powerful wine gradually softens and mellows over time. Generally speaking, you should open vintage port when it is about twenty years old, although tastes vary and some prefer their port much older than that. A mature vintage port should have masses of plum, fruit cake, chocolate, berry fruits, and more but should still be soft enough to enjoy easily, perhaps with a chunk of mature hard cheese. You may need to decant it before drinking to remove a sediment. Lesser styles include late-bottled vintage (LBV) from not-so-good years, and single-*quinta* – from one estate. From a reputable producer, these can provide excellent value. Then there's tawny port, which tastes quite different, as it's long-aged in oak barrels for a mellow, nutty style that's delicious lightly chilled. And don't forget Madeira, the fortified, "cooked" (heated) wine from the island of the same name. There are four styles of quality Madeira; we recommend you try the driest, Sercial, served chilled as an apéritif, and the sweetest, Malmsey, at room temperature for sipping by the fire.

Spain

The land of sherry. The area around Jerez, in southern Spain, produces white wine from the Palomino grape, which is then affected by a natural yeast coating called *flor* that gives it a salty tang. Pale, dry, crisp fino and manzanilla are the result. These are among the best apéritifs in the world. Drink them cold and fresh, perhaps with salty snacks, to sharpen the taste-buds before a big feast. Oxidized/aged versions of sherry are known as amontillado (usually medium-dry) and oloroso (richer, older, and often sweeter, although do look out for rare but delectably dry olorosos). Very sweet sherries can be crass and cloying, especially the cheaper cream styles, but the almost treacly, dark, PX style (made from Pedro Ximénez grapes) is irresistible when poured over ice-cream (honest). Overall, sherry remains a high-quality, well-priced, classic wine. It's just a pity so many underrate it.

And the rest...

Sweet wines are made all over the world. Try the following, rarer examples if you get the chance:

- **Canadian Icewine** All the crisp acidity and luscious sugar of the best European dessert wines.
- **Austrian dessert wines** Top examples are made near the shores of the Neusiedlersee, where the lake mists rise regularly, creating the right conditions for botrytis. Mainly graded for sweetness as German wines. The best are Rieslings and Grüner Veltliners.
- **New Zealand** A few sweet wines are made on both islands and they are great, although all too rarely seen abroad.
- **South Africa** South Africa still makes some old-fashioned fortified sweet wines. Again, rare, and standards vary considerably among producers.
- **Other Italian and Iberian sweeties** To name but two, these include Marsala, the sweet fortified wine made in Sicily, which tastes of toffee and nuts; and Moscatel de Valencia, the commonly seen and fair-value sweet Spanish wine.

Making the most of sweet wines

Serve all lighter, golden sweet wines lightly chilled. Stickier, richer, amber/ruby-coloured styles, like Australian liqueur Muscat or red port, are better at room temperature. Pour small quantities of dessert wine – because it has intense flavours, it is for sipping rather than quaffing!

WINE & FOOD MATCHING

Matching food with wine is not quite like matching a pair of shoes or socks. There's no right or wrong about it; it's just that some combinations are more enjoyable than others. It's like cooking: some partnerships – tomatoes and basil, grilled fish and lemon, strawberries and cream – just gel. In the following pages you'll find suggestions that should act as starting points – safe choices and more experimental ones – so give them a try and see if they work for you. The great thing is that you never stop discovering new and exciting combinations. Just as you improvise with recipes, one day you'll try out an unfamiliar wine with a dish and *Eureka!* It'll be a perfect partner.

Mastering the basics

Put simply, light food suits light wines, and robust, gutsy food calls for robust wine. A guideline that's far handier than the old "white wine with fish, red wine with meat" rule.

Six key food flavours

Salty

Inherently salty foods such as anchovies and oysters go best with crisp, dry white wines such as Muscadet and Chablis, and with tangy manzanilla sherry. Neutral whites also go well with salt beef and salt cod. Add salt to food to make oaky reds seem less tannic.

Sour/sharp

The taste of lemon, lime, or vinegar can be quite difficult to match with wine. A wine with a good level of acidity of its own, such as a Sauvignon Blanc, Riesling, or a light Italian red like Valpolicella, tends to work best. Squeezing lemon juice onto a dish can also make full-bodied whites or reds taste less oaky.

Savoury

The kind of flavour you find in mushrooms, soya, smoked meats like bacon, aged Parmesan, and concentrated meat reductions – referred to by the Japanese as *umami* – is the best kind of match for medium- to full-bodied reds. Also good with vintage Champagne.

Spicy

Food spiced with chillies or peppercorns reduces the sweetness of any wine that accompanies it, so it can make dry reds like Bordeaux taste quite astringent. It also accentuates obvious oak flavours. Go for unoaked or lightly oaked wines with juicy fruit.

Smoky

Smoked foods need a wine with a strong enough personality to cope with their powerful flavours. Dry fino or manzanilla sherry is generally a safe choice but, oddly, a touch of sweetness can work well, too. German Kabinett Rieslings are good, for example, with smoked fish and meats, especially pork. With smoky barbecue sauces it's best to choose a powerful red wine such as a Shiraz or a Zinfandel.

Sweet

Sweetness in a dish makes any wine seem drier. Sweet wines should always be sweeter than the dessert or they'll taste thin and sour. With savoury dishes that contain fruity or sweet elements such as honey, or a cranberry or lingonberry sauce, that isn't always possible but at least make sure your wine is one that has some good, lush fruit of its own.

Soups & starters

Think of starters as mini versions of main courses, although somewhat lighter, fresher wines will generally work better at this stage of a meal. Soup is often better without wine, unless the soup in question is quite thick and chunky. But here's what works if you do want to try adding wine.

DISH	SAFE BETS	ADVENTUROUS ALTERNATIVES
Thin soups and broths	Classic Rhône or modern Languedoc white-grape blends (spicy, flavourful mixtures of Roussanne, Marsanne, and Viognier grapes)	If it's an Asian-inspired soup or broth, try New Zealand Sauvignon Blanc or an Australian Verdelho
Thick, chunky soups like minestrone	If there are a lot of green vegetables it, try a dry Italian white like Soave. If it includes tomato and garlic or beans or lentils, go for a robust southern French, Italian, Spanish, or Portuguese red	A dry Spanish *rosado* (rosé)
Seafood soups and stews like bouillabaisse	Generally best with crisp, dry whites – the kind you find in Provence and elsewhere in southern France – or with an inexpensive Sauvignon Blanc	Picpoul de Pinet: a dry, Muscadet-like wine from the Languedoc in southern France. Or a Spanish Albariño
Chowders and other creamy soups	Unoaked or lightly oaked Chardonnay or South African Chenin Blanc	Viognier or New World Pinot Gris
Gazpacho and other cold soups	Inexpensive Spanish whites such as unoaked white Rioja. Or, if you're willing to spend a bit more, try an Albariño	Well-chilled fino or manzanilla sherry

Sherry

Traditionally paired with soup, bone-dry, well-chilled fino or manzanilla sherry is equally good with seafood. Try it with smoked salmon, squid, or fried or grilled fish – and, of course, tapas such as olives, nuts, air-dried ham, and spicy chorizo sausage.

Salads & eggs

Salads determine your wine choice only when they're the main course – not when served as a side dish. As light, summery foods they call for crisp, dry whites and rosés, although a punchy dressing calls for a more gutsy wine. Eggs and wine can be surprisingly good; contrary to popular belief, there are some delicious matches to be made.

Salads & dressings

DISH	SAFE BETS	ADVENTUROUS ALTERNATIVES
Light vegetable and seafood salads	Sauvignon Blanc works well, particularly if the salad contains asparagus. Rosé is ideal with salade niçoise	Dry English whites
Caesar salad; salads with chicken or cheese	Unoaked Chardonnay or Chardonnay/Semillon blends. South African Chenin Blanc	Modern Italian whites like Fiano
Tomato, mozzarella, and basil; other antipasti salads	Dry Italian whites such as Pinot Grigio, Soave, Orvieto, and Verdicchio	Spanish Rueda; unoaked white Rioja
Asian flavours: spicy dressings	Off-dry Australian Riesling, Semillon, or Verdelho	Argentinian Torrontés; Austrian Grüner Veltliner
Warm salads with duck or pigeon breast or chicken livers	Young New World Pinot Noir works particularly well. California and New Zealand provide the best value	German or Austrian reds
Gutsy salads with grilled vegetables or a spicy or garlicky dressing	A soft, medium-bodied red such as Chilean Merlot	Fruity Californian Zinfandel

Eggs

Unoaked or lightly oaked Chardonnays go well with omelettes and many other egg dishes. Try Alsace Pinot Blanc, Soave, or sparkling Chardonnay/Champagne with egg dishes, too, switching to light, fruity reds with ham and eggs or eggs with a tomato sauce.

Pasta & rice

Pasta is such a regular part of our diets today that we usually grab whatever bottle is to hand to match it. Still, a bit of thought pays off. Pair creamy, light, vegetable (*e.g.* asparagus) and fishy pasta dishes with whites, and tomato- or meat-based ones with red. Always match the wine to the sauce, not the pasta shape! For rice and grains, as with pasta, the way they are cooked should determine your choice. Many rice dishes are representative of an ethnic cuisine, so be guided by the cooking style.

Pasta & noodles

DISH	SAFE BETS	ADVENTUROUS ALTERNATIVES
Spaghetti carbonara and other creamy sauces	Soave, Bianco di Custoza, Pinot Bianco, unoaked Chardonnay	Inexpensive Viognier
Spaghetti alla vongole and other fishy sauces	Dry Italian whites such as Pinot Grigio or Frascati	Unoaked Greek whites match the feisty fishy flavours with a zip of their own. Or try Chilean or Californian Sauvignon Blanc
Spaghetti al limone	Verdicchio dei Castelli di Jesi, Orvieto	Valpolicella
Pasta alla genovese (with green pesto)	Gavi, Soave, Bianco di Custoza, inexpensive Chardonnay	Albariño (from Spain). With red pesto you'll probably enjoy a soft, medium-bodied red like Merlot more
Bolognese and other meaty pasta sauces	Decent Chianti, good Valpolicella	Californian Zinfandel, Côtes du Roussillon and other southern French reds; Tempranillo from Spain
Napoletana and other tomato-based sauces	Montepulciano d'Abruzzo, Barbera	Hungarian Merlot
Puttanesca and other gutsy sauces with anchovies, olives, or capers	Sicilian or southern Italian red such as Negroamaro	Argentinian Bonarda or Syrah

(Continued overleaf)

DISH	SAFE BETS	ADVENTUROUS ALTERNATIVES
Lasagne, cannelloni, and other baked or stuffed pastas	It depends what they're layered or stuffed with. If they're meaty, go for the same type of wine as for Bolognese (see page 137). With spinach and ricotta, try a dry Italian white like Soave. Or, if the dish is based on mushrooms, a light Italian red like Dolcetto	With spinach: trendy Spanish white, Albariño. With mushrooms: Californian or New Zealand Pinot Noir
Polenta	Light Italian reds such as young Nebbiolo or Dolcetto	Chilean Carmenère or Merlot

Noodles

Most noodle dishes are based on Asian flavours, so tend to suit assertive New World wines best. White grape varieties like Sauvignon Blanc, Semillon, Verdelho, and Riesling work well, particularly from Australia, where this type of food has charmed its way into the culture. Austrian Grüner Veltliner is a fashionable choice with spicy food. And if the dish forms part of a Chinese meal, try a fruity rosé.

Rice & grains

DISH	SAFE BETS	ADVENTUROUS ALTERNATIVES
Risotto	Most dry Italian whites. If made with red wine, try Dolcetto. Or Valpolicella	With spring veg: Sauvignon Blanc. With shellfish: unoaked Chardonnay. With mushrooms: Pinot Noir
Paella	Spanish rosé; unoaked white Rioja; Tempranillo	Rhône or Languedoc whites or rosés
Biryani and pilau	Unless accompanied by other hotter dishes, any inexpensive dry white or rosé	Indian sparkling wine; cava; Viognier
Sushi	Green tea and miso soup	Champagne or other fizz; Muscadet and (we're assured by a Japanese friend) red Burgundy

Fish

Most fish has a delicate flavour that isn't going to overpower any wine. Many dry whites work, so your choice may be determined by the occasion and how much you want to spend. Introduce ingredients such as tomato and garlic or lime and coriander, or use the grill or barbecue, and you'll need wines that will stand up to stronger flavours.

DISH	SAFE BETS	ADVENTUROUS ALTERNATIVES
Fine fish like halibut, turbot, and sea bass	Chablis, white Bordeaux, Sancerre, Pouilly-Fumé, or unoaked or subtly oaked Chardonnay	Champagne
Salmon	Unoaked or lightly oaked Chardonnay	For seared or chargrilled salmon: Pinot Noir, Cabernet Franc, and other light reds
Mackerel, sardines, and other oily fish	Sauvignon Blanc	A sharp-flavoured, lemony Greek or Portuguese white
Tuna, shark, and other "meaty" fish	Australian, Chilean, or New Zealand Sauvignon Blanc or a Sauvignon blend. Unoaked New World Chardonnay	Pinot Noir, Cabernet Franc, and other light reds
Fish cakes and pies	Inexpensive Chardonnay	Good Burgundy or top New World Chardonnay
Barbecued or spicy fish	Sharp-flavoured, lemony whites, dry rosés, light reds	With "meaty" fish, try a Shiraz or Merlot
Trout	Light Chardonnay	Dry German Kabinett Riesling
Shellfish	Unoaked Chardonnay; Chablis; Muscadet	New World Sauvignon Blanc or Riesling. Champagne for oysters and lobster
Smoked fish	Riesling and authentic pale dry sherry. (Kippers and wine are disgusting)	Champagne is a classic with smoked salmon, but good dry German or Austrian Riesling is more interesting
Fried fish	Sauvignon Blanc, Muscadet, and Pinot Grigio, but, if fried in butter, Chardonnay is better	Bubbles are brilliant – try cava

Meat

If it's meat, it must be red wine, right? Well, more or less. There is nothing better than a good red wine with most meat dishes. But, like other ingredients, the ideal match also depends how you cook it – and there are dishes where white wine is just as enjoyable an option.

DISH	SAFE BETS	ADVENTUROUS ALTERNATIVES
Beef and steak	Most reds go with simply cooked beef. Red Bordeaux is classic, but almost any good medium- or full-bodied red – particularly Cabernet Sauvignon, Merlot, and Syrah – will do	Madiran or Uruguayan Tannat; Argentinian Malbec; red wines from the Douro in Portugal
Raw beef dishes like carpaccio or steak tartare	Italian reds such as Chianti Classico	Provençal rosé; vintage rosé Champagne
Homely dishes: meatloaf, casseroles, and stews	Southern French reds like Fitou, Corbières, and Côtes du Roussillon; cheap Sicilian, Spanish, and Portuguese reds	Moroccan reds – made in much the same style as those in the South of France
Veal	In general, veal goes with similar types of wine as pork. Italian-style dishes such as scaloppini and osso buco work well with dry Italian whites	Try a Pinot Grigio or Pinot Gris from Australia, New Zealand, or California
Grilled and roast lamb	Mature, oaky reds such as red Bordeaux and Chianti; Spanish reds such as Rioja and Ribera del Duero; Merlot and inexpensive Cabernet	Greek reds; traditional southern Italian reds such as Copertino and Salice Salentino; the famous Lebanese red, Château Musar
Lamb shanks and other braised lamb dishes	If cooked in wine, drink the same or a similar wine with the dish	Characterful, medium- to full-bodied French red such as Côtes du Roussillon or Crozes-Hermitage. Or Argentinian Malbec
Roast pork in white wine or with apple sauce or cold	Dry whites; roast pork with apple sauce and cold roast pork work well with Chardonnay or Chenin Blanc	If you prefer a red, drink a good Beaujolais, Côtes du Rhône, or fruity Merlot

DISH	SAFE BETS	ADVENTUROUS ALTERNATIVES
Pork with cream and mushrooms	Lightly oaked Chardonnay	Viognier; Alsace, New Zealand, or Oregon Pinot Gris
Stir-fried pork; sweet-and-sour dishes	Fruity whites such as Australian Semillon	Australian or Argentinian rosé
Spare ribs	Rich, full-on reds like Chilean Cabernet or Californian Zinfandel	South African Pinotage
Sausages	Sausage dishes suit rustic southern French blends of Syrah, Grenache, Cinsault, and Mourvèdre; also Spanish reds	You can find these grape varieties Down Under, too
Ham, gammon, and bacon	Chablis, unoaked Chardonnay, Merlot, Beaujolais	Australian Semillon

White wines with meat

Examples of white wine and meat combinations include: Australian or Alsace Riesling with Thai beef salad; Mâcon-Villages Chardonnay with boiled beef; Sauvignon Blanc with grilled lamb marinated in olive oil, lemon juice, and garlic; South African Chenin Blanc with cold roast pork; Reserve Californian Chardonnay with steak; and – not white but pink – rosé Champagne with rare roast lamb.

Charcuterie

French-style charcuterie (saucisson, pâté, rillettes, and terrines) goes with Beaujolais and other French country reds (Gamay, Merlot) or dry southern French whites. Italian-style (salami, prosciutto, etc.) goes with dry Italian whites: Valpolicella, Dolcetto, or authentic red Lambrusco. Spanish-style (serrano ham, chorizo, etc.) goes with fino or manzanilla sherry, Spanish *rosado*, unoaked white Rioja or other dry Spanish whites.

Barbecues

Powerfully sweet, smoky barbecue sauce can kill delicate wines. Instead, stick to reds with plenty of juicy fruit – but not too much oak or you'll get an overload of charred, spicy flavours. Some good reds to try are: Australian Shiraz, Californian Zinfandel, Chilean Cabernet, Argentinian Malbec, South African Pinotage.

Curries

All except the hottest curries can be successfully paired with wine. Mild kormas go well with many different styles, including crisp, dry whites and rosés, but on the whole you'll find a ripe, fruity red like Merlot or Carmenère will do the job best. Young Rioja is also good with lamb curries.

Cold or hot?

Cold meat suits lighter (and cooler) wines than hot meat dishes, so when you automatically reach for a chilled red or rosé in summer you'll find it hits the spot perfectly.

Chicken & other birds

Where to start with chicken? There are so many different ways of cooking it that you'll have to match virtually every flavour in the book. Two wines that will generally cope are Chardonnay and Pinot Noir.

DISH	SAFE BETS	ADVENTUROUS ALTERNATIVES
Plainly roast or grilled chicken	Red or white Burgundy or other Chardonnays or Pinot Noirs	Chianti or other light, fruity Italian reds
Chicken kiev and other fried chicken	Sharp, citric whites like Sauvignon Blanc; unoaked Chardonnay; light reds	Pinot Grigio
Chargrilled chicken with herbs or salads	Provençal or Languedoc rosé has the right feel	Spanish rosado from Navarra; Semillon or Semillon/Chardonnay
Poultry with creamy, white wine, or cheese sauces	Unoaked or lightly oaked Chardonnay; Alsace Pinot Blanc; New Zealand or Oregon Pinot Gris	Viognier, Roussanne
Chicken cooked in red wine, like coq au vin	Red Burgundy is traditional but Rhône reds work well, too	New World wines from the red Burgundy grape: Californian or New Zealand Pinot Noir
Sweet-and-sour or fruity chicken dishes	Fruity whites such as Semillon, Semillon/Chardonnay, and Australian Riesling; light, fruity reds	Australian Tarrango
Chicken in smoky barbecue sauces	Australian or South African Shiraz	Zinfandel; Argentinian Malbec; South African Pinotage
Chinese-style sweet-and-sour chicken dishes and mild curries	Australian Semillon/Chardonnay	Bordeaux or other Merlot-based rosé
Turkey/Goose	Turkey: white Burgundy or New World Chardonnay; soft, fruity red such as St-Emilion Goose: Barolo or Pinot Noir	Turkey: Australian sparkling red Goose: quality German or Alsace Riesling, or Gewurztraminer
Duck	With simply cooked roast or pan-fried duck, Pinot Noir in the form of light red Burgundy. If a fruity sauce is involved, more robust New World Pinots	If the duck is cooked with orange, off-dry German Spätlese Riesling, or Australian Semillon. With duck confit or duck with olives: robust, rustic reds from the South of France

Vegetables

It's the cooking that counts. Raw and lightly cooked vegetables generally call for light-bodied white wines. Vegetables cooked with a creamy or cheese-based sauce work well with Chardonnay, and chargrilled or roasted vegetables tend to go well with red wines.

VEGETABLE	SAFE BETS	ADVENTUROUS ALTERNATIVES
Artichokes	None. Artichokes are a notorious wine-killer, particularly with red wine	Italian whites such as Orvieto or Verdicchio dei Castelli de Jesi will just about see you through
Asparagus	If served with a (not too acidic) vinaigrette: Sauvignon Blanc; if served with a hollandaise or butter sauce: unoaked Chardonnay	Dry Muscat or Alsace Riesling. With chargrilled asparagus and Parmesan, light reds can work
Aubergines	Rustic reds such as Fitou, Côtes du Roussillon, or Sicilian reds	Moroccan or (especially for moussaka) Greek reds. Zinfandel. Crisp, dry whites and rosés with cold dishes such as baba ganoush
Mushrooms	Unoaked Chardonnay or a good Pinot Noir	With wild mushrooms, serve a top red Burgundy or a Californian or New Zealand Pinot Noir
Peppers	Southern French and Spanish reds such as Côtes du Roussillon-Villages, Côtes du Rhône, and young Rioja. Dry rosés	Sauvignon Blanc works surprisingly well
Pumpkin or butternut squash	Choose wine with some character: Californian Chardonnay or Viognier; Shiraz	Dolcetto, good Valpolicella
Tomatoes	Raw: Pinot Grigio and other dry Italian whites; Sauvignon Blanc. Cooked: southern French, Spanish, and Italian reds; unoaked Syrah	New World Sangiovese, Sicilian reds

Herbs, spices, & seasoning

It might sound far-fetched to choose a wine to go with a herb or spice, but some flavours and seasonings have a real affinity with a particular grape variety or style of wine. Don't be nervous about drinking wine with spicy food – unless it's very hot indeed (*see* page 148).

SEASONING	SAFE BETS	ADVENTUROUS ALTERNATIVES
Basil (particularly pesto)	Dry Italian whites such as Soave, Bianco di Custoza, Gavi, and Lugana; light, unoaked Chardonnay	New World Pinot Grigio
Coriander (fresh) and dill	Sauvignon Blanc	Australian Verdelho
Mediterranean herbs: thyme, rosemary, oregano	Rustic reds like Côtes du Roussillon and Corbières	Greek reds
Mint	Try Cabernet Sauvignon – it has a real affinity with mint	Dry whites such as Sauvignon Blanc are better with Middle Eastern-style dishes
Tarragon	Unoaked Chardonnay	French blends of Roussanne, Marsanne, and Viognier; Arneis
Garlic (as in chicken kiev or garlic butter)	Sauvignon Blanc or inexpensive unoaked Chardonnay	Barbera and other Italian reds
Ginger (especially in oriental dishes)	Aromatic whites such as Alsace or Chilean Gewurztraminer; Riesling; and, curiously, Champagne	Champagne or other sparkling wine
Mustard (as in rabbit with mustard sauce)	Dijon mustard is the most wine-friendly type and goes well with lighter Burgundies – white and red	Unoaked Chardonnay; Rioja *reserva*
Paprika/*pimentón* (as in goulash)	Tempranillo; Syrah; southern French reds	Eastern and central European reds, *e.g.* Kékfrankos
Saffron (as in paella, risotto milanese, etc.)	Dry Italian whites such as Soave; Spanish *rosado* or young Tempranillo	Spanish Albariño

Fruit & fruit puddings

The cardinal rule is that your wine should be sweeter than your dessert – which makes fruity desserts the easiest to match, and cold ones easier than hot ones. Also, chill the wine to counteract the sweetness of the food.

DISH	SAFE BETS	ADVENTUROUS ALTERNATIVES
Apples and pears: simple tarts	Almost any light, sweet wine will do. Sweet Loire wines; sweet Bordeaux	New World botrytis Semillon works particularly well
Peaches and nectarines: fresh or poached	Sauternes and cheaper options such as Monbazillac and Saussignac, and Muscat de Beaumes-de-Venise	*Demi-sec* (medium-sweet) Champagne
Strawberries	Moscato d'Asti; Premières Côtes de Bordeaux; late-harvest Semillon (if served with cream)	Light, fruity reds such as Beaujolais are delicious poured over strawberries
Fruit salads	Moscato d'Asti or Asti	Sweet Riesling or Gewurztraminer
Apricots	Muscat; late-harvest Riesling; Tokaji if served hot	Spanish Moscatel de Valencia
Raspberries	Late-harvest Rieslings (better still if you add cream)	With raspberry sauce or coulis: raspberry liqueur topped up with Champagne or sparkling wine
Blackberries, blackcurrants, and blueberries	Sharpness makes them tricky. Late-harvest Rieslings go best	Coteaux du Layon from the Loire
Gooseberries	Very good with Muscat de Beaumes-de-Venise	For a non-alcoholic alternative, try elderflower cordial
Lemon-flavoured desserts	Very sharply flavoured lemon tarts are hard to match, but sweet Rieslings should cope	Icewine (Eiswein) – but it's *very* sweet!
Orange-flavoured desserts	Inexpensive French or Spanish Muscat	Greek Muscat from Samos
Pineapple and other tropical fruits	Late-harvest or botrytis Riesling or Semillon	Jurançon from southwest France

Chocolate & other sweet things

Drinking a sweet wine with something as sweet as chocolate or with creamy desserts might seem like too much of a good thing, but the experience can be so sublime you should occasionally indulge.

DISH	SAFE BETS	ADVENTUROUS ALTERNATIVES
Creamy desserts (crème brûlée, panna cotta, light cheesecakes…)	Sweet Bordeaux, especially Sauternes; late-harvest Semillon	A southern French Muscat
Light, airy desserts (soufflés, creamy gateaux, and roulades)	Sweet (*demi-sec* or *doux*) Champagne	Sparkling Vouvray
Caramel-, toffee-, and nut-flavoured desserts	If light, like crème caramel or an almond tart, an inexpensive Muscat should work. With richer desserts such as pecan pie or sticky toffee pudding, try an Australian liqueur Muscat	Ten-year-old tawny port
Honey-flavoured desserts	Inexpensive Muscats – so long as the dessert is not *too* sweet	Australian liqueur Muscat
Chocolate	None – especially with dark, rich, molten chocolate desserts, but sweet red wines such as Black Muscat, Mavrodaphne of Patras, and Recioto (a sweet Valpolicella) are OK; Banyuls and Maury (French *vins doux naturels*) work reasonably well, too	Orange Muscat can be good with white-chocolate or milk-chocolate desserts
Hot puddings (bread-and-butter pudding, Christmas pudding)	Inexpensive dessert wines, such as Greek and southern French Muscat	Hungarian Tokaji; Passito di Pantelleria

Ice-creams & sorbets

Only really rich, viscous wines like liqueur Muscat (great with toffee crunch ice-cream) or sweet oloroso or PX sherry (try with vanilla) really work.

Cheeses

If you've ever wondered why your favourite wine doesn't go with the cheese you're eating, the answer is that cheese and wine aren't the miracle match they're made out to be. So if you're a cheese-lover and have piled the board with a huge selection of different cheeses, watch out!

CHEESE	SAFE BETS	ADVENTUROUS ALTERNATIVES
White or bloomy rind cheeses such as Camembert and Brie	So long as the cheese isn't too ripe: soft, fruity reds such as Chilean or other New World Merlot; Californian or New Zealand Pinot Noir; good Valpolicella	Dolcetto or Loire reds such as Bourgueil and Saumur-Champigny
Hard cheeses such as Cheddar, Lancashire, and traditional English cheeses	Medium- to full-bodied reds without too much tannin: Rioja, St-Emilion, and softer styles of Bordeaux; good-quality Côtes du Rhône-Villages, Shiraz/Syrah, and Grenache	Oaked Chardonnay can be surprisingly good
Blue cheeses	Inclined to be troublesome partners for any wine, apart from the classic partnerships of Roquefort and Sauternes, and port and Stilton	Hungarian Tokaji; Australian liqueur Muscat; ten-year old Madeira; Mavrodaphne of Patras (a sweet red wine from Greece)
Strong, smelly cheeses	None. Better kept away from your best bottles, particularly fragile old Bordeaux and Burgundy	Again, sweet or fortified wines are likely to do best of all. Or aromatic whites, as in the traditional pairing of Munster and Gewurztraminer. If you still want a red, try one with a touch of porty sweetness, like an Amarone
Very rich, creamy cheeses such as Vacherin	Not easy. Try Californian or New Zealand Pinot Noir	Young Grüner Veltliner or a Swiss white
Goat's cheeses	Sauvignon Blanc is a stellar match, but English dry whites or Sauvignon Blanc-style whites from Spain will go well, too	Light, fragrant Cabernet Franc-based reds from the Loire, such as Bourgueil, Chinon, and Saumur-Champigny

(Continued overleaf)

CHEESE	SAFE BETS	ADVENTUROUS ALTERNATIVES
Sheep's cheeses	Robust southern French reds such as Corbières, and wines made from the Syrah, Mourvèdre, Grenache, and Tempranillo grapes	Corsican or Sardinian reds. Or a sweet southern French Muscat
Smoked cheeses	No totally safe bet!	Morio-Muskat; other inexpensive Muscats

Cheese before or after dessert?

Whether you have your cheese French-style (before dessert) or after is a matter of choice, but it is one that can also depend on the wine and the cheese you're serving. If you're drinking a good red, it makes sense to follow the main course immediately with cheese, but if you're serving cheeses like Roquefort that go better with a sweet or fortified wine, you may prefer to leave them till the end of the meal.

Potential wine-killers

Problems for wine are created by ingredients that are unusually sweet, sour, hot, or salty, such as habanero and Thai bird's-eye chillies; vinegar, especially sharp vinaigrettes; horseradish, wasabi, and English mustard; pickles and chutneys; raw garlic (or onion); truffles; and salted anchovies.

Chillies

Very hot chillies cause problems for wine, but crisp, fruity whites such as Sauvignon Blanc are OK. The dried chillies in Mexican or southwest American food are better with more full-bodied Chilean or Californian reds such as Cabernet Sauvignon.

Truffles

Truffles are highly scented and have an overwhelming influence. Black truffles go with the sort of wines that work with game: red Burgundy and aged Barolo. White truffles are good with vivid, young Italian reds (like Dolcetto) and fabulous with mature vintage Champagne.

WINE & HEALTH

Drink a little wine and it could be good for you – but drink too much and it might well be very harmful. These facts are rarely addressed in books about wine, so this chapter aims to answer some frequently asked questions: How much is too much? What is sensible drinking? Is drinking in moderation really good for me? Can I drink when pregnant? Much of the information here has come from Alcohol in Moderation (AIM), a non-profit organization that seeks to promote sensible consumption of alcohol, working with academics and doctors on its council. For more information, visit www.drinkingandyou.com or www.aim-digest.com

General facts

Many people enjoy drinking wine, and for the majority of us drinking in moderation should not cause any problems. As we shall see, there can even be health benefits. Yet drinking too much can be harmful. Sensible drinking is knowing where the benefits end – and the risks begin.

Although there's no reason why most people can't enjoy some wine as part of a healthy lifestyle, it helps to know the limits. The British government defines sensible drinking as three to four units for men and two to three units for women a day (where 8g/10ml/¹⁄₃oz of *pure* alcohol equals one unit). However, be aware that recommendations, and the definitions of what constitutes a unit, vary from country to country (the examples in the table below show the range for what is generally medically accepted as "moderation"). In any case, it's important to note that these recommendations are daily totals; don't "save up" your units for a Saturday night binge. In fact, the World Health Organization recommends spreading the number of units you drink throughout the week, with two alcohol-free days per week.

But what is a "unit" when it comes to wine? Don't make the mistake of thinking that one glass of wine is one unit of alcohol; it's not nearly so straightforward. A small 125ml (4¹⁄₄oz) glass of wine at 12% ABV is 1.5 UK units (or nearly one US unit). But that's "small" indeed, when compared to the much larger 175ml (6oz) or even 250ml (8¹⁄₂oz) glassfuls commonly served these days. And wine of 12% ABV is only moderately powerful. Many wines (particularly those from warm "New World" regions) weigh in at 13–14.5% ABV. So if you down a glass of stronger wine from a larger glass, the units mount up quickly. A 175ml (6oz) glass of 14% ABV wine is nearly 2.5 UK (or 1.6 US) units.

Look at the alcohol level of your wine (it must be stated somewhere on the bottle). Some wines are naturally much lighter than others. German Riesling, for example, is often relatively low in alcohol, and completely delicious to boot. And watch out for larger glass sizes when estimating your units. A few bottles carry unit information on their labels, helpfully, and some wine outlets now even display the unit content of popular drinks on their shelves.

Country	Source	Standard unit of alcohol	Recommended intake	Total
USA	Federal dietary guidelines	12g	Men – 2 units Women – 1 unit	24g 12g
Spain	Ministry of Health	10g (spirits = 17g)	Men – 3 units Women – 2 units	30g 20g
UK	Dept. of Health	8g	Men – 3–4 units Women – 2–3 units	32g 24g

Effect of alcohol on the body

So how does alcohol enter the system, and what happens to it once it has been absorbed? Here are the key answers to these questions – and some good news for all those who love claret!

An enzyme in our stomachs, known as alcohol dehydrogenase (ADH), is key to breaking down alcohol. Women's stomachs contain only about sixty per cent as much ADH as men's, which is why women's daily drinking guidelines are lower than men's. Blood-alcohol level (or blood-alcohol concentration, also known as BAC – the amount of alcohol in the blood) is related to the rate of drinking, as alcohol is absorbed into the bloodstream from the small intestine. The alcohol is then transported in the bloodstream to the liver, which breaks it down.

The capacity of the liver to break down alcohol is limited, so that if there is more alcohol in the liver than it has capacity to break down, the remaining alcohol circulates in the blood, reaching other organs and tissues of the body, such as the brain. The alcohol remains circulating until it has all been broken down by the liver (which can manage about one unit an hour of alcohol, generally speaking). With the aid of ADH, alcohol is converted in the liver into toxic acetaldehyde, which is then broken down into water and carbon dioxide, substances that are excreted via the body's "natural route".

The fact that alcoholic drinks in moderation, especially wine, help prevent gastro-intestinal infections has been known for a very long time. Claret, as drunk by the British army in India, was held to be "a sovereign preventative against the prevalent cholera". The antioxidants are believed to help prevent infection by *Helicobacter pylori* bacteria. Wines and other alcoholic drinks may also inhibit *E. coli*, salmonella, and others.

The effects of fizz

Sparkling wines do indeed "go to the head" more quickly than other table wines, but this is not because they are stronger. It's because of the bubbles. These increase the surface area of the wine, so the alcohol is absorbed more quickly. In fact, at around 11–12% ABV, most Champagnes and sparkling wines have slightly lower alcohol levels than many still table wines.

The morning after

Don't automatically blame port, sherry, and other stronger fortified wines when you have a hangover after a huge feast. Some ordinary table wines are over 14.5% ABV, while the weakest fortified wines (dry pale sherry, usually) are not far off that, at around 15.5% ABV. So if you downed a lot of red and white, your hangover can't entirely be explained by the small glass of port or sherry you enjoyed at the end of the meal!

J-shaped curve

Now for the good news: light and moderate drinkers of any form of alcohol tend to live longer than those who abstain or drink heavily. This widely accepted relationship is commonly known as the "J-shaped curve", and it makes happy reading for those who enjoy one or two drinks from time to time.

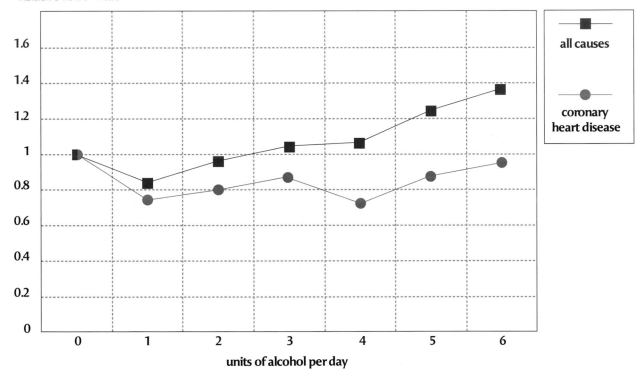

As the graph shows, the relative risk of mortality is lowest among moderate consumers (*see* the lowest point of the shallow-J-shaped curve). It is greater among abstainers (the left-hand side of the J), and much greater still among heavy drinkers (the right-hand side). In addition to longevity in general, the J-shaped relationship also exists for cardiovascular deaths, and specifically for coronary heart disease, which is the leading cause of death in the Western world. For this reason, a great deal of research into alcohol's risks and benefits has focused on cardiovascular disease. Read on...

Wine & the heart

As the J-shaped curve graph shows, moderate wine-drinkers (rather than teetotallers or heavy drinkers) would seem to have some protection from cardiovascular disease. Indeed, studies consistently show that regularly drinking moderate amounts of alcohol reduces mortality from coronary heart disease by between twenty-five and thirty per cent.

It is thought that the alcohol itself accounts for most of the protective effects in drinks, by altering the balance of fats or lipids in the blood via stimulating the liver to produce the "good" high-density lipoprotein cholesterol (HDL). Alcohol also helps to stop red blood cells sticking together, or clotting – a major cause of heart attacks and strokes.

So the good news is that regular moderate wine drinking may reduce the risk of coronary heart disease and stroke, especially in men aged over forty and postmenopausal women. It is in these groups that the risk of these conditions significantly increases. But this applies only to normal healthy adults: don't drink alcohol if you have uncontrolled high blood pressure. It is also recommended that you seek a doctor's advice if you have an existing heart condition.

Much has been written on the health benefits, particularly to the blood and the heart, of the "Mediterranean diet": one that is high in fruit, vegetables, fish, salads, olive oil, and red wine. Certainly, many people who enjoy wine also seem to enjoy plenty of these foods in their diet. One particular study (the Lyons Heart Study) found that this type of diet, combined with moderate wine drinking, did indeed help prevent a second heart attack in middle aged men. Compared to non-drinkers, men enjoying two glasses of wine a day reduced their risk of a second heart attack by nearly sixty per cent. It is possible, though, that wine-drinkers simply have more moderate lifestyles; there's some evidence, for example, that wine-drinkers tend to be non-smokers, well educated, and more moderate in their habits.

Antioxidants also play a part in the cardio-protective effects of wine. Specific phenolic or antioxidant compounds and their polyphenolic forms account for the other twenty-five per cent of wine's protective effect. Resveratrol and quercitin, antioxidants found in wine, are more powerful than even vitamins C and E. Because these are mainly found in the skin of the grape, red wine has a much more concentrated amount of antioxidants than white. (Dark beer has more than light beer, too.)

Stopping "bad" cholesterol
Antioxidants work by preventing "bad" cholesterol from accumulating on the walls of blood vessels, and by enabling those walls to relax and dilate, which can help prevent strokes. They also work by decreasing the clotting together of red cells. Now you know.

Wine & pregnancy

Which wine-loving mum-to-be has not agonized about whether she can have a drink during pregnancy? Although a (lucky) few simply go off the stuff (sometimes developing a metallic taste in the mouth when drinking wine), for many women this presents a dilemma, not helped by the confusing information that abounds.

If you drink when you are pregnant, alcohol from your blood crosses the placenta and enters the baby's blood. Drinking during pregnancy can affect the development of the foetus. In the first three months, heavy drinking can damage its developing organs and nervous system. After this, continued heavy drinking can have the additional effect of stopping the baby from growing and developing properly. Foetal Alcohol Syndrome (FAS) is the name given to a set of rare but serious problems in babies whose mothers drank very heavily throughout pregnancy. These include facial deformities, poor growth, and mental problems.

Scary stuff. So does this mean you have to stop? For many, this is the easiest option, and there is no doubt that giving up completely during pregnancy is a sensible decision. However, UK government guidelines suggest that it is safe for healthy pregnant women to drink just one or two units once or twice a week. If you do drink occasionally during pregnancy, make sure you stick to a small glass or two (a 125ml/4¼oz measure, not a 250ml/8½oz bucket), and try to choose wines that are naturally lower in alcohol, such as a light Riesling.

Those trying to conceive should stick to the same guidelines. Drink only one or two units once or twice a week; otherwise the alcohol could interfere with menstrual and fertility cycles. Men should also note that drinking heavily lowers the sperm count.

Breastfeeding: the express route
We know that alcohol clears from a mother's milk at the rate of about one unit every two hours. So if you're breastfeeding and allergies aren't an issue, then one small glass of wine should be perfectly OK. But do avoid more alcohol before you breastfeed – or express some milk and save it for your baby if you'll be drinking later.

Wine & allergies

When is a bad reaction to alcohol an allergic attack, and when is it merely a hangover? Too much is made of wine and allergies – after all, it is almost certainly the amount of alcohol that made you ill – but these reactions can occur.

A food or drink allergy occurs when a normally harmless substance is perceived as a threat by the body's immune system. In a few sufferers, even light alcohol consumption can cause an allergic reaction. Allergic reactions include migraines, itchiness, rashes, asthma, and swollen eyes. If you suffer these symptoms when you drink wine, see your doctor.

Many people think the main cause of allergic reaction to wine is sulphur dioxide, which is used as an antioxidant and preservative in almost all wines. However, unless you have a similar reaction when eating dried fruits such as apricots, which have much higher levels of SO_2, this is unlikely.

What about yeast allergy? A very small amount of dead yeast remains in a finished wine. This is such a tiny amount that it should not affect the vast majority of people. But if you have a yeast intolerance, and suspect that wine is aggravating this, then make sure to avoid styles that are aged *sur lie* – on the yeast for extra complexity and flavour. These include Muscadet *sur lie*, many Champagnes and premium sparkling wines, and sherry.

If you have a simple hangover, you need to drink plenty of water, the main problem at this point is dehydration, especially of the brain cells. The way to prevent a hangover in the future is, of course, to drink less alcohol, but also be sure to pace yourself, eat when drinking, and make sure you take in plenty of water alongside your wine.

Do organic wines prevent allergic reactions and hangovers?
No, unfortunately. Organic wines (*see* page 78) are usually made with less sulphur than non-organic wine, so if you have a sulphur intolerance, choose organic. But organic wine, of course, still contains alcohol – the main cause of sickness after heavy drinking.

Frequently asked questions

There are other factors to take into account when drinking, such as your age, whether you are driving, special medical conditions, and the fact that wine is fattening. Here are the answers to some posers.

Q: When should I avoid drinking wine altogether?

A: It's best not to drink and drive at all – or, if you must, do remain well within the drink/drive limit for the country you are in. Don't drink and operate heavy machinery, use electrical equipment or work at heights. Be careful if you are taking certain medications; always check with your doctor if unsure. Don't drink before exercising strenuously or swimming.

Q: What about the very young and the very old? Can they drink safely?

A: Under British licensing laws, sixteen- and seventeen-year-olds are allowed to drink beer, wine, or cider during a meal with adults on licensed premises. Over-eighteens are allowed to buy their own drinks. It is illegal to give an alcoholic drink to a child aged under five, except under medical supervision in an emergency. It's important to teach teenagers about responsible, moderate drinking and to explain certain issues such as "spiked" drinks, which, sadly, they may encounter. As for the elderly, moderate drinking can help prevent heart conditions, as explained on pages 154–5. And there is some evidence that moderate wine drinking can help reduce the risk of dementia and Alzheimer's disease. But heavy drinking is clearly harmful, causing neural damage and memory loss.

Q: Can wine cause cancer?

A: Yes and no. Moderate drinking has been linked to a reduction in cancer mortality rates (of as much as twenty per cent, according to a study by the American Cancer Society in 1998). This evidence was found in those drinking two to four units a day. One reason for this is thought to be the antioxidants found in grape skins. But the risk of cancer increases at consumption levels above moderate levels. There is certainly no doubt that prolonged heavy drinking increases the risk of many cancers. And there is a link between breast cancer and drinking, with no safe level of consumption yet established.

Q: I'm a diabetic. Can I still enjoy wine?

A: Depending on the severity of their disease, diabetics can enjoy alcohol in moderation and preferably with food. Unsurprisingly, drier styles of wine are recommended, and high-sugar styles such as dessert wines, liqueurs, and fortified wines should be avoided.

Q: Is alcohol fattening?

A: How can dry wine be fattening, when it contains no fat and very little sugar? In fact, wine does contain calories. A small (125ml/4¼oz) glass of dry wine has approximately ninety-five calories. Sweet or more powerful wines contain much more.

Glossary

See also "Touring the World" (pages 42–65) for further useful definitions.

ALCOHOL BY VOLUME (ABV) How much alcohol (expressed as a percentage) is included in an alcoholic beverage. Another way of specifying the amount of alcohol is "proof".

APPELLATION CONTROLEE (AC/AOC) French wines made to the strictest standards, with rules governing grapes, soils, yields, alcohol, and vineyard source. Generally a sign of premium-quality wine, although there are exceptions.

BARRIQUE A 225-litre oak barrel, used to ferment/age wine.

BIODYNAMICS Extreme form of organic viticulture, which looks at effects of planetary movements on vines. (See page 70.)

BOTRYTIS See page 21.

BRUT "Dry." Seen on Champagne and sparkling wine labels.

CLASSICO Italian term denoting that a wine – for example, Chianti or Soave – has been made in (supposedly) the best part of a designated zone.

CRIANZA Spanish wine that has been barrel-aged for one year. *Sin crianza* means "unoaked".

CRU Literally "growth" in French. Refers to a single estate or property, or a specific, usually highly rated, vineyard area. *Cru classé* is a growth from the Médoc's five-tier classification system. *Grand cru* is the top category of named vineyard site; *premier cru* the second-highest.

CUVEE A simple way of referring to a batch of wine. A Champagne house might make a dry, non-vintage *cuvée* and a special anniversary *cuvée*. A New World producer is more likely to use the term "bin", as in bin number.

DEMI-SEC Medium-sweet.

DO/DOC/DOCG Refers to wines made under controls, less strict for DO but more so for DOC and DOCG in Portugal, Spain, and Italy (DOCG is Italian only). Like AC, a general indication of quality, premium wine, but no guarantee.

DOUX Sweet to very sweet.

FLOR Literally "flower" in Spanish. A yeast that grows on sherry, which stops oxidization and adds flavour.

GRAN RESERVA See Reserva, below.

LATE HARVEST/VENDANGE TARDIVE Sweeter, riper-tasting wine made from grapes harvested later than the normal time. These are sometimes botrytized (nobly rotten).

METHODE TRADITIONNELLE The Champagne method of making sparkling wine. Wine is bottled with a little yeast and sugar and it is this second fermentation in the bottle that results in bubbles trapped in the wine.

MIS EN BOUTEILLE PAR... French for "bottled by..."

NOUVEAU New wine, usually very light and simple, just released from a recent vintage. Meant to be drunk young.

QUALITATSWEIN Means "quality wine" in German, but don't expect all bottles marked thus to please. QbA (bestimmter Anbaugebiete) indicates premium wine made in a specific region of Germany, while QmP (mit Prädikat) is of a special quality based on sugar levels.

QUINTA Portuguese farm or estate.

RESERVE/RESERVA/RISERVA "Réserve" has no legal meaning in France. In Spain, Portugal, and Italy however, "Reserva" and "Riserva" refer to wines that have been aged longer before release. Often the best wines are kept back for barrel-ageing. *Gran reserva* (usually Spain) means even longer in cask/bottle.

SEC/SECCO/SECO "Dry".

SUR LIE Aged on the yeast sediment (lees) and bottled directly from it, without racking or filtering.

TERROIR French term for the environment in which grapes are grown, *see* page 80.

TROCKEN German term for "dry".

VIN DE PAYS See page 51.

VIN DE TABLE/VINO DE MESA/VINHO DE MESA/VINO DA TAVOLA Basic table wine from, respectively, France, Spain, Portugal, and Italy. Quality ranges from ordinary to poor, but you might come across the odd gem.

Index